ANYTHING I EVER REALLY NEEDED TO KNOW I LEARNED FROM

ANIME

ANYTHING I EVER REALLY NEEDED TO KNOW I LEARNED FROM

ANIME

BY SID NARGED

Published 2008 – Sid Narged – www.sidnarged.com

10 9 8 7 6 5 4 3 2 1

ISBN-13: 978-0-9793080-3-1
ISBN-10: 0-9793080-3-8

Dedicated to Happy Bacon and Laird D's Disciples

Kevin (my clone)	*Eggs (for Pres)*	*eD (ah!)*
Barlow (Gimpy)	*Monkey (el presidentè)*	*Cornwallis (Otaku)*
Bucci (Believe it!)	*Yoshi (the ninja)*	*Carlo (you're weird, but cool)*
Captain Planet (crunk)	*Marquito (the Cuban)*	*Ray "the man" Stacy*
Drew (Jason)	*Xiao Yuan (Derek)*	*Ashley Abreu*
Dan Barron (WOOO!)	*Dave Lima (WOOO!)*	*Mr. Sensitive Ponytail Man*
Zotnix (lolcatbible.com)	*Anonymous*	*Dickie (ewok)*
Beato the Frito Bandito	*Friggin' Riggan*	*Gameboy*
The Cambodian	*Dick Mitten*	*Marshmallow*
Loren (scabies)	*The Lesbian (scabies)*	*Midget (Econo-Lodge)*
The Joslin Twins	*Jorgel (What if...?)*	*Nancy (4 toes are fine)*

And everyone else that I forgot because you were just too cool…uh yeah.

*Special Thanks to Hamster for the artistic consultation
and Sawyer for the typo-detection system.
(Blame her if you find one... I personally think it adds character!)*

TABLE OF CONTENTS

INTRODUCTION

It doesn't matter what you call it. It is life to some people. It's currently called Anime, however when I was first introduced to it in my youth, I had no such moniker for it. It was just cartoons.

The truth is that anime is what it is; a representation of a story. Some good, some bad, some really, really bad... long, short, deep or shallow... fantasy or reality... there are lessons to be learned. Like a new age Aesop's Fables, with ninjas, mechs (giant robots), cat women, teenagers, hormones, and even tentacles; these are stories that bring up issues that are learnable, recognizable, and very much usable in everyday life.

As this book progresses, you must keep in mind some of the realities of life that are unusually well demonstrated in anime. In life as in anime, there are exceptions to every rule, the only constant is change, there are no guarantees in life, and women with unnaturally colored hair (no matter the color) have a certain allure to them. (Why do you think women color their hair?)

I have been following the anime world for more than 25 years; it was called cartoons when I was little, became Japanimation in my teens, progressed to anime, and is now a phenomenon that encompasses the world. Originally, the only people that I remember, who knew or cared about these cartoons were people like me; people who weren't so comfortable in their own skin. We were the D&D players, the video gamers, the chatters, and the geeks...

This book explains the lessons to be learned from anime; some are easy to apply, some fanciful and unusual... others are surprisingly simple. I hope that the anime culture will embrace this book, as your culture is one that has allowed this proliferation of stories, from which all of these lessons were learned... viva the otaku!

THE BASICS

CHAPTER 1

We learn that things go a whole lot smoother if we have a good understanding of the basics. These basic rules are the core of what living is all about.

NOTHING IS CERTAIN.

There are exceptions to every rule, and therefore nothing is certain - including this rule. You may find situations in life where you believe that you understand everything. You never know. This doesn't mean that you should give up, or stop trying to figure things out, but you can never be certain about anything.

DON'T LIE - ESPECIALLY NOT TO YOURSELF.

Life is complicated enough without having to sort through all of these illusions and delusions we call lies. Lies can cause people to get hurt, whether or not the truth is ever revealed. Nice people usually lie to themselves about their own ambitions and emotions, and bad people usually lie to others to attain their own ambitions.

EVERYONE AND EVERYTHING WILL EVENTUALLY DIE.

This is nothing to worry about, everything dies. Life is a short endeavor in the scheme of things, and though the physical body may die, the actions you take in life will live on after your death... for better or worse. Make good things happen in life. Help others and you will be remembered, hence you will live on after you are physically gone.

HAVE A GOOD SENSE OF HUMOR.
It's better to laugh at yourself than to be angry at the world. It may take a little time and a little getting used to, but people with a good sense of humor tend to have less pain in life. They can see the humor in things and, even in a bad situation, seem to have an advantage. Everyone has flaws, don't hate yours, they are what make us unique.

SHARE WHAT YOU HAVE.
There's no point in having anything without the ability to share it with others. What's the point of feeling love if you don't share it with the one you love? There are people who have very little and share all that they have, and they are appreciated by all of those who they come into contact with. There are others who appear to have everything, but are miserable because they have no one to share it with. You can get a lot for a little if you share.

DON'T BE AFRAID TO ADMIT WHEN YOU'RE WRONG.
A lot of pain and suffering comes from those who just won't admit that they are wrong - even when they know that they are wrong. Many times they do things that they know are wrong out of spite, just because they can. It takes a far more intelligent person to admit that they are wrong and learn from a situation - it also shows character.

THE ONLY CONSTANT IS CHANGE.
Time changes everything, and time never stops, so everything is in constant change. Accept change as necessary, but it's not completely beyond your control. Change happens, but it doesn't

mean that things need to change in a bad way; you can effect change. Be prepared for change, it keeps life interesting. Even though many times change causes pain, change should be viewed as generally positive; things are happening and that is good.

RESPECT YOUR ELDERS.

Life is a journey, and the elderly have been on the road for a long time. They have seen things you haven't seen, done things you haven't done, and lost more than you've ever had. This experience is the source of their power. Even if their body seems frail, and their mind twisted or perverted, there is a certain respect to be given to those who have been through so much in life. They are your future - and besides, they may just know enough to be able to hurt you with little effort. They may be old and strange, but they are powerful by the virtue of time itself... respect them.

PROCEED WITH CAUTION.

Everything is fragile, and can be easily broken or destroyed if we aren't careful. People's feelings, lives, self confidence, relationships, families, possessions, and futures can be irreversibly altered with little interference. Think before you act - your life is just as fragile. Be careful. You never know the damage that a single action can do until it's too late. This doesn't mean don't act, because that can sometimes be worse than doing the wrong thing - but proceed with caution.

LOVE WITH CONVICTION.

Love is a strong emotion, and when it happens, it's best if it's not taken lightly. Time is short and unrequited love is a terrible thing - seize the moment. Embrace your love and follow it with conviction. There is nothing better in life than love realized - but you need to first realize it exists before it can come to fruition. Do so with cautious confidence; it can be torture, but the rewards are great.

NOTHING IS IMPOSSIBLE.

Some things seem impossible, but this is a fallacy. Anything can be done with enough effort, ingenuity, innovation and manipulation. However, this doesn't mean that it *should* be done. It may seem impossible to drag the one that you love away from the one that they love, but that's not the case. You can do anything, but at what cost. All of the great unknowns can be conquered, but perhaps some of them are better left unknown.

FOLLOW YOUR HEART AND DREAMS.

You can live your entire life doing what others tell you to do, and get praise for it, but in the end it may mean nothing to you, because those weren't your dreams. Use your efforts to follow your dreams. There are times when you may not know if you are right or wrong, but follow your heart - at least then you are doing what you feel is right. Maybe you fail at making your dreams come true, but at least you have made the effort for yourself - and it is better to try and fail at a dream, than to succeed in a reality that you don't believe in.

THE GREATER THE RISK, THE SWEETER THE REWARD.

The best things in life require effort and a certain risk of failure. You have to risk loss to gain the rewards that are worth living for. Taking the personal risk may make you vulnerable to failure, but also leaves you open to accept the greatest gifts that can be given. The one who risks most has the most to lose, but also has the most to gain. This isn't always something tangible like life or property, but the things we hold most dear - our own feelings, fears and pride.

THE FANTASY

Anime is a representation of stories and fantasies portrayed for entertainment. They wouldn't be nearly as entertaining if their topics didn't induce fantasy in the minds of the viewers. Some of these fantasies are universal - others are not.

FALLING IN LOVE WITH A CHILDHOOD FRIEND.

This is a story that can be told with many different variations; it can be a lifelong childhood friend or a friend you were separated from in your youth. They could have been taken away, or your family moved away. You may have made a childish promise to them that you would never forget them, or that you would get married when you're older. These are very common stories.

You then start having feelings for someone you've known for as long as you can remember, but you've always just thought of them as just a friend. This can cause all kinds of confusion and chaos, making great stories - especially depending on the portrayal.

THE MYSTERIOUS STRANGER FANTASY.

Another wonderful fantasy is that of the stranger. It's a fantasy everyone can have because it involves the random chance of running into someone who you don't yet know. That's the beauty of it. This could be a foreigner, an exchange student, an alien, a stalker, or just a person you bump into on the street. Many of these fantasies invoke interesting emotions and the possibility of falling in love at first site.

These stories will probably exist till the end of time, especially considering the unlimited ways you can run into a complete stranger, and that is what makes them so interesting. How will they meet? Will it turn out ok in the end? Who knows? But it makes a great story.

BEING NURSED BACK TO HEALTH.

Some people have a tendency to get injured. Maybe they aren't that tough, or maybe they live a tough life. Some people suffer from a frail and weak constitution. No matter how it is approached, these people need love too; and how better to give these people love than to give them someone who can care for them when they need it most. This is a good fantasy for everyone. We all want someone who cares for us when we are sick or hurt; it's an easy fantasy to associate with.

To care for someone in their time of need is a showing of love and devotion. Whether a stranger or someone you know, it's good to fantasize about the ones who care for you, when you can't care for yourself.

THE DAMSEL (OR DUDE) IN DISTRESS.

Heroes and heroines are great fantasy plot elements. They are strong, bold, cunning, and usually somewhat misunderstood. To save the one that you love may mean sacrificing your life for them. This risk is what makes these stories so popular. To risk your life, to save the one that you love, shows that you care for them more than yourself; a true representation of the power of love.

Very entertaining plot points that allow for action, suspense, and courage are also good ways to establish and define people's feelings toward one another. Great stuff.

THE GIRL NEXT DOOR.
There seems to be this deep infatuation with the concept of either living somewhere or moving next to a person they find attractive. This doesn't need to be a direct neighbor. This could be someone in your apartment building, next door, or nearby. The closer they are, the better the fantasy.

THE HOT SPRINGS GETAWAY.
Hot springs are a natural wonder of this planet and to be caught in an encounter in such a romantic place is a fantasy with surprising complexity. Some people are very self conscious about their bodies and this is a place where that concept gets challenged, along with the ability to restrain oneself from complete giddy perversion. This battle of trying to maintain is what makes these awkward situations so embarrassing and humorous, as well as being very eye opening.

THE BEACH VACATION.
There's something about the natural wonder and beauty of the ocean, mixed with a healthy helping of exposed flesh that makes the beach vacation fantasy so appealing. The pure uninhibited playfulness also helps. To be able to enjoy the sand and surf like a small child, while dealing with the awkward glances of those who are attracted to you, also makes this vacation one to remember. There are few situations more beautiful than being with the one you love on a beach, with the moon reflecting off a calm sea. The sheer romantic vision allows for all kinds of possibilities - for the heart, mind, body and soul alike.

THE SHY ONE BECKONS.
There's something to be said about being shy. There's a certain mystique about it. A person who doesn't interact well with others seems to be a challenge to some. Maybe you should try and approach them and bring them out of their shell, or try to figure out why they are so introverted. There are a lot of

questions surrounding the shy person. Do they not like me? Do they not like anyone? Do they think I'm too ugly to talk to? It's possible that they are just shy, and the shy person has trouble talking about their thoughts and feelings. Common yet cute.

THE BLOSSOMING BEAUTY ARRIVES.

An interesting fantasy is the finding of beauty in a place you didn't know it existed. Maybe a girl who has grown into herself or a girl who had such poor fashion sense that it made her appear undesirable. Maybe it's just someone you never really thought about in that way before, and when it comes to light, it changes everything. To have been so close to this beauty and not even realize it for so long... this is a story that's a beauty in itself.

THE OPPOSITE OVERLOAD.

There's a fantasy for many young boys that has been in existence for many lifetimes. What would you do if you were somehow the only male in a place full of females? This has many different manifestations; from the tropical island, to the planet of the Amazon women. This fantasy is sometimes portrayed in anime, and sometimes it's a major plot point. It's an almost universal fantasy; however the approach of this situation being more of a curse than a blessing is an interesting twist, and frequently portrayed as such.

CATS FIGHTING OVER THE SCRAPS.

Just like men want to show their love, and women want to see it expressed, there's a small piece of everyone that wants to be wanted; and also to see if someone likes you more than anyone else. This can sometimes cause battles to happen; though somewhat unpleasant to think about, having it out with someone over the person you both want is a major fantasy for some. For a woman, it's to see two guys fighting and competing for her affection... and for the guys, well, sometimes just seeing two girls go at it is enough. Usually men would just assume watch the fight than care who's winning.

WIN OVER THE CRUSH.

Everyone has had a crush from time to time in their lives, which makes this fantasy element so universal; and so often the crush goes unfulfilled and unnoticed. Sometimes the crush even ends in a hurtful denial. The great part about this anime world, is sometimes, the crush wins the affection of the person they have a crush on - something we've all contemplated and wished for, but is so rarely realized.

MAGICAL MOMENTS.

True magic is difficult to come by in the real world, but there are still magical moments that we all share. Some forces that we come up against seem to be more powerful than the forces we are normally used to. Where this may not be magic, like we see in the fantasies of anime, we sometimes wish we had magical powers to make things happen when they seem impossible. If only we could fly, transform, see the future, teleport, be invisible, or see through clothes... I mean walls... maybe the situations in life would seem more magical. However, we can make magic moments of our own anyway... you just need to believe.

TO COSPLAY OR NOT TO COSPLAY - WHAT THE HECK IS COSPLAY?

Speaking of taking fantasy into the real world, there's always cosplay. What is cosplay you ask? Think of it like what the Trekkies have been doing for years - dressing up like your favorite characters and hanging out with other like-minded goofballs. Now there are arguments for and against cosplay or costume-play, but you have to answer that question for yourself. Are you the person who's so obsessed with a certain character that you want to dress and act like them? Are you comfortable enough with yourself that you can dress that way and still respect yourself in the morning? Do you think that it makes it easier or more difficult to meet people when you're dressed up like someone that you're not? Or do you just want to have a hell of a good time, escape reality for a while, and live out some of your fantasies? Any of these are good reasons to cosplay.

Now I'm not going to get into a dispute over cosplay, but it is a fairly popular phenomenon; it's fun to watch and it isn't hurting anyone. But I do have a point that I want to pose to the anime community that most people just don't talk about too much.

Personally, I think that if you dress up like a character, you should at least have some physical attributes that are similar to the character you are dressing up as. Now there are people out there who will argue that there aren't a lot of fat girls in anime, so that rules them out. I guess that depends on the anime you watch, but I think we can all agree that the fat 45 year old guy should not be dressing like a 14 year old school girl. Do what you want - but I had to say something.

THE NOT SO HAPPY ENDING.

The truth hurts, and in life, as in anime, things don't always have a nice happy ending. It seems that, even with fantasy, there are problems that can't be overcome. It's sad to say, but sometimes it just doesn't work out... and that's just fine. It adds a little extra realism to the story if there's a little bit of an upset. The perfect ending is nice, but sometimes it's fake, and even though we all want a happy ending, we can accept the not so happy ending as well. That's life.

LOVE

Love plays a big part in life, and is a big part of the stories we find in anime. Some of the greatest stories are about this wonderfully complex emotional bond between two people or two... whatever things happen to be in love. The point is that love is recognizable to us at a very primitive level... as love can transcend life, and everything else...

LOVE IS FICKLE.

People, who fall in love easily, often do it frequently. Love is an enigma. Those stricken with quick love (i.e. love at first sight) can sometimes change direction with their love on a dime, and without hesitation, move onto their next love interest. This seems to be the shotgun approach to love. You're hunting for the love that loves you back so, love everyone who interests you! This method is often fraught with misery however, as love, even love generated rapidly, can cause disappointment. Especially considering that the person who loves you most likely will not be in the initial shotgun blast, and they will feel alienated (sometimes, very alienated), jealous, or otherwise pissed off at watching you love all these other people.

LOVE IS STRONGEST FROM THOSE CLOSEST TO YOU.

This does not just mean physically close, but it sure does help. There are those that make your heart race, and you can't get out of your mind, out of your life or even out of your sight. There is the realization that sometimes even those who you find obnoxious, timid, strange, freakish, or even alien, have a way of working their way into your heart - if they are around enough.

LOVE DOES STRANGE THINGS TO YOU.

How do you recognize love? Well, just as everyone is different, there are many different manifestations of love. Of course there are a few good indicators. Your heart races, maybe you get a little absent minded or clumsy. Blushing and never getting that person out of your mind are a few good indicators for yourself, but it's much harder to see true love in other people. This will make you feel unsure of yourself sometimes, because it's difficult to be in love when you can't see the love blatantly returned to you.

Love can take the sure and make them insecure and confused, as it can take those who are confused and make them see clearer than they ever have. It can calm the restless, and introduce chaos to the logical. It can change you in ways you never thought possible. It can make a pacifist kill, and turn a killer into a kitten. Meow.

REPRESSED LOVE BLOSSOMS THE PRETTIEST FLOWER.

Many times when you start to fall in love, you don't recognize it, accept it, or admit it; so you push those feelings deep down inside. This can many times cause that feeling to resurface later, a little bit stronger. This is love trying to let you know that it's there. You can try and try, but until you admit it to yourself, you're just going to be miserable. However, since this is love, when you finally do admit it to yourself, it will tend to bring completely different miseries along with it; but at least you're being honest with your feelings.

You can fight those feelings all you want. You may both be fighting them. You can hate your feelings, fear your feelings, even hide your feelings... but if you explore the possibilities, you may just find something more beautiful than you could have possibly imagined; and it was right in front of you the whole time.

LOVE KNOWS NO BOUNDS.

There are no boundaries to love at all. Time, space, gender, race, age, species, obstacles, and inanimate objects are all fair game. It's difficult to say if this is because the many different ways that love can manifest itself, or if we just label all of these good feelings under the same love umbrella, but that's just the way it is. Love is unpredictable. You can hate someone one minute and love them the next. It can overcome any obstacle, and you cannot contain it. The only thing you can do is recognize it.

Some people love those who they feel are unattainable, unacceptable, undesirable, or just plain weird. There are no reasons for love sometimes. It's a feeling - an emotion. Love is not always something straight forward and simple. There are many different types of love. You can love many different people and things without loving them "that way."

We love family, friends, pets, nature, plants, possessions, and even ideas... but that just shows the many different complexities of love. You can love someone without being in love with them, and this can complicate life for all those concerned.

Love can blossom from the fruits of the forbidden. You can be told that something is bad and wrong, and in your search for your own reasons to hate it, you find something different. Our curiosity and emotions can cause strange and wonderful things to happen.

Even though love can overcome all of these boundaries, it is still a fragile and complex thing. Many people reject feelings of love because of the pain that can come with it and the sincerity that is needed to maintain it. There are those who fear it, those who embrace it, those who aren't ready for it, and those who jump too soon into it. Love can overcome many things, it just may not occur the way you had expected.

THE FIRST KISS ISN'T EASY.

The first kiss is almost always an awkward undertaking. Sometimes there is hesitation, delays, disaster, interruption, self-consciousness, or even a bloody nose. The more horrendous the anticipation, the better the first kiss will be. However, this doesn't always means you've won. Sometimes the first kiss can go off without a hitch, but then there are the same misfortunes when trying to get a follow-up kiss.

The lesson to be learned here is self-confidence; brazen, unabashed self-confidence. There are too many unsure things in this world, if you want to capitalize on your first kiss; you need to be sure of yourself. Don't hesitate; if you miss the moment through hesitation and self-doubt, you may never forgive yourself.

You can attempt to over-plan these things. The trick is to be flexible and spontaneous, but to act with calculated resolve. You can do it. Just go for it. No doubt. No fear. You can try to make the perfect situation for the first kiss; but life doesn't work that way. Learn this now - it only takes both of your lips and the one you love. Screw everything else.

GOOD BOYS, BAD BOYS AND THE WOMEN WHO LOVE THEM.

Trying to understand what women want is impossible, unless you realize that they want it all. She wants a good boy that cares for her, a bad boy who makes her want him, and a friend who is just like her, but not too much like her. This is a tough thing as a single person, but this is how you can pull it off.

Be good and caring in your heart. This is harder than it seems. You need to able to give this part of yourself to someone, which can cause pain if you give it to the wrong person. Be open-minded, and find the one who can give their heart back to you.

Be strong. Women see the bad boy as desirable because they show their strength and, to a woman, strength is good. Strength of character, mind, and body, as well as control over action is a good way to show women that you are not a pushover. You don't have to win every fight; this is a misconception. Strength of character in defeat can be a better indicator of worth than someone who wins every battle.

Be a little mysterious and a little insecure. Even if you've known her forever, don't just spill every insecurity you have about everything. You need to let her know that even though there are things that you are not sure about, and things she may not know about you… you are sure about your feelings for her. This balances well with the insecurity and mystery. The only thing she needs to know is that you are sure about how you feel…

Women want a man who can give them a little bit of everything. This is not always monetary or material, but is more like a rollercoaster… life and love are not very interesting without their ups, downs, loops, and turns. Run hot… run cold… women want to have a bear and a wounded puppy… Someone to fight with, fight for, and fight against.

JEALOUSY IS INSECURITY.

Everyone has insecurity. No one can live life completely secure about everything, but it does give a good indication of how someone feels. Remember that jealousy and envy are two different things. Jealousy is about something you have, that you're afraid to lose or have taken away; and envy is wanting something that someone else has. If you are jealous, you have made the assumption that what you have is not secure, and that you care if it leaves. If you were secure that nothing could ever happen, then there would be no jealousy - but you have to care about that possibility, if you care about that person.

Jealousy is complicated further by envy. Envy can drive someone to want what you have, and then try to take it away. You need to understand the threat to your security, and jealousy can be your friend. Sometimes people are jealous for no reason... mainly their own insecurity; however, jealousy can be a great early warning system for when an envious person is trying to take what you have.

EVERYONE HAS A BREAKING POINT.

Women... you have good reasons to be jealous. Men can be fickle, and sometimes have a very low level of self-control. If you see another woman going after your man... get in there and kick her ass! Men have self-confidence issues, and this generally means that they can be swayed if they are feeling a little unappreciated.

Men... your main reason for jealousy is not because you are with a tramp... which is entirely possible. Your main reason for jealousy is that you know the envy of men, and how hard they will try to get your woman. If your relationship is good and strong, she probably will not be leaving you for another man, but if you are slacking off in your relationship... BEWARE!

Everyone has a breaking point; a time when feelings for a person are no longer being sustained by the relationship. This is a reason why people move on after a relationship ends. If the person you loved dies, there is no more relationship to sustain it. There is no shame or dishonor in moving on. A person who doesn't show you love in your relationship is also not a good place to be... remember guys... there's nothing wrong with showing your love to the person you love.

In the end, relationships are ours to screw up, and we will screw them up. You probably will feel love and loss and then feel love again... maybe even for the same person. Cherish it while you have it, and good luck...

MEN AND GIRLS, WOMEN AND BOYS.

Age difference and love can be strange. It's not so much the feelings are different, which they can be, but the perception is different. It seems the rule of thumb is, within a few years either way is acceptable. As you age the gap may increase a little, perhaps up to 25 percent deviation, based on the older person and the circumstances involved... after that, it's just plain creepy.

I am not saying that it's impossible to swing outside of that, for every rule has its exceptions (especially in anime), but as a rule we don't have a lot of 400 year old hotties hanging around, hitting on the guys who are 18. Maybe this rule should be amended to being a perceived age.

This is the same in the real world... but as in anime, there is a double standard... to a point. Wrinkled old men and pretty young girls are a common celebrity occurrence, but if a woman wants a younger guy, she better be in good shape. It's just the way of the world. Young women can get away with a distinguished older man on the basis of security and safety... also he's less likely to find a better option at his age. He can take care of her and she can... um... take care of him.

However, an old woman with a young guy seems to go against the laws of nature. Men are supposed to be the strong providers for their women... not playthings of elderly women; unless she looks like a young woman.

LOVE IS A DOUBLE STANDARD.

Love for someone immediately creates a double standard. You will allow someone you love to get away with things that would be considered unforgivable, if they were perpetrated by someone you didn't love. This is one of the reasons why love is considered somewhat dangerous. But this double standard also works to create strong bonds in the relationship. You will offer more time and attention to someone you love. This may alienate those outside the relationship, but it is a necessary and acceptable side-effect. This is generally where jealousy can come in from the previous relationships. Family and friends can become jealous that they have been put on the back burner; envy can creep in from those outside who see how much time you are spending together, and the relationship can isolate the couple from other outside influences.

This willingness to treat someone you love differently from other people is the double standard. You have a standard for your love that is different from those you don't, and this can be taken advantage of, even with true and just intentions.

RELATIONSHIPS

CHAPTER 4

Many people spend a great deal of time, effort and money trying to start, maintain, and understand relationships. Since everyone is different and a relationship involves two, this complicates things further. Here are some interesting lessons about relationships.

YOU CAN WANT HER, BUT IF SHE DOESN'T WANT YOU... YOU'RE SCREWED.

It seems like a simple lesson. Everyone understands that relationships are two people wanting to be with one another... you can't force that. Sure you can manipulate her, convince her, persuade her, or just plain win her over... but you can't force her. Every woman is different, so good luck finding out what's going on in her head - she probably doesn't even know.

YOU CAN WANT HIM, BUT IF HE DOESN'T WANT YOU... YOU CAN PROBABLY PULL IT OFF ANYWAY.

Here's another simple lesson. Men are a whole lot different than women. Sure men want who they want, but they also want who they can get. It's an interesting difference. This would make you assume that it's easier for a girl to get a guy... and you're right... but it's also easier for other girls to get him. So where it may be easier in the beginning, it can be a different story to maintain.

It may be difficult to keep up, and he may go astray, but it's a slightly better situation than the guys, who get nothing for their unrequited love. Women get all the breaks.

GIRLS CAN SOMETIMES FALL FOR THEIR FRIEND'S BOYFRIEND.

A somewhat complex aspect of the female psyche is the part that falls for their friend's boyfriend. This is compounded by the fact that they don't want to hurt their friend's feelings or relationship. They may just see the relationship as something that they wish they had. Women contain a great deal of envy. They want things that others have that make them happy, under the assumption that the same condition will be passed to them if they attain it. It is further complicated by a woman's inherent empathy towards emotion. They can almost feel their friend's love for their boyfriend, so that emotion then becomes transferred to them.

This doesn't always result in a failed relationship, but it can sometimes strain the friendship, as confusion, competitiveness, and distrust can easily get in the way. This does occur sometimes, but it's not always acted upon. Sometimes that emotion is stored and it comes back in a time of weakness in the relationship... or a breakup.

Women have a pretty simple mechanism in place to make it so they don't usually act on this while the relationship is strong and healthy - it's called common sense. First, it can hurt a friendship that may be very important to them. Second, if he would cheat on your friend, what would keep him from doing that to you once you get him? Finally, he's already had his way with your friend, which means sleeping with him would be like sleeping with all the guys she's been with... and you know she's a tramp, she tells you everything.

GUYS CAN SOMETIMES FALL FOR THEIR FRIEND'S GIRLFRIEND.

This is not a terribly complicated aspect of the male mind - men like women. Men enjoy the chance to get to know any girl, and their friend's girl is almost obligated to talk to them. Men are always looking for an opportunity... and they don't have the same qualms with taking their friend's girl (et tu, Brute?).

For men it's just about the girl, not about the friend... it's not even about her feelings so much. This selfish, ego-centric attitude sometimes infects guy's minds and they just act on instinct. Taking your friend's girl may seem a little extreme for some, so there's always plan B - the girlfriend's friends; who do not want to hurt their friend's feelings... so it's the perfect plan. Be available, be nice, and put up the appearance that you can do the same for her as he has done for their friend. I know it's complicated, but the driving force behind it is simple - get women.

GUYS WANT GIRLS WHO CAN COOK.

One of the things that guys look for in a girl is the ability to cook. This seems to be more than just a lazy guy thing. Guys want their women to have all kinds of traits that will make them happy - and men like to eat. A girl who can cook is a long term investment for a male. Long after they're married, have kids, and don't have the same spark that they used to, he will still enjoy that she cooks for him to make him happy. Not to mention that someone who can cook is almost like a status symbol, and something to be proud of; "oh yes, she's pretty, smart, and a great cook – so there."

This actually helps in the selection process. A man who has a few different options may choose the one who cooks for him, just because he sees that she would be a better long term choice. Maybe the way to a man's heart is through his stomach after all.

GIRLS WANT A GUY WHO WILL TAKE THEM OUT TO EAT.

Most women understand that a guy wants a woman who can cook - however, many men have not yet figured out that they have to do their part as well. Women do not like having to cook all the time. Every so often the guy needs to take her out somewhere. If you think about the real world here for a second, a relationship usually starts out with dating, which usually involves going out to eat somewhere; it doesn't usually start out with the guy saying, "I like orange flavored beef, spicy and medium rare. Hop to it, toots."

MEN WANT LONG TERM RELATIONSHIPS TOO.

As it so happens, guys really do like the stability of a long term relationship - no one likes to go home alone. There's no good point to being a good protector and provider without having someone to protect and provide for. Men may, in many cases, be less sociable than women, making it difficult for them to have anyone to share their experiences with. However having a woman there who understands you, comforts you, and accepts you for who you are - makes life that much sweeter.

The big drawback to this is that men have problems with long-term commitment. It's not that they don't want a relationship to last; men just don't like putting guarantees on anything. They'll try, but they know that they are flawed - so putting that type of guarantee on a defective product seems silly to a guy.

A woman can keep a guy faithful in a long term relationship without this commitment though; just make him love you more than anything else in the world - including himself - then you win. Figuring out how to do that is the hard part.

WOMEN WANT LONG TERM COMMITMENTS.

Unlike men, women can be 100% sure of their fidelity in a relationship. Their resolute stubbornness can guarantee that they can commit, so they expect the same. Women don't generally dump their emotional commitments as lightly as men do. This means that, before they invest all their emotions in a relationship, they want a commitment of some sort. Women don't usually open up completely until after this commitment is reached, or at least a token gesture is made.

This can complicate things further by leaving the man in the dark about what her real feelings are - making him less likely to commit. It's almost a catch 22. If she puts herself out on a limb, without commitment, she risks getting hurt - but if she doesn't put it out there, he may not commit.

MEN ARE FROM EARTH, WOMEN ARE FROM - WHO CARES? THEY'RE WOMEN!

Women are foreign creatures to men. Men don't understand why women do what they do, however men are usually more primitive in their thought processes - closer to earth in a way. Women have different things that trigger their moods and actions than men. It would seem on the surface that women want to be loved, cared for, and supported - and man is more of a conqueror. Ugh - woman!

WOMEN LIKE GAY MEN.

Many women in this world would appreciate a man who is more in touch with their feminine side, however that tends to be a difficult feat for a man; no one can be everything to everyone. A man is not interested in doing many of the things women want to do - but gay men seem to have a different relationship with women. Maybe it's because they both love the same thing - this brings gay men into an intimate state of understanding with the woman's difficulties of dealing with men in a relationship. A gay man has the unique perspective of loving men, being a man, and not being threatening to women. I can see how this would be an excellent companion for a woman... and he'll tell her exactly how she really looks in that outfit.

She doesn't generally feel sexually attracted to the concept of a man and a man together, but it's more of a friend who can see things from their point of view.

MEN HAVE A LOVE/HATE RELATIONSHIP WITH LESBIANS.

There is a somewhat different relationship when it comes to men and lesbians. Most men don't enjoy the fact that lesbians pose them a risk of not getting a female. Men are generally boneheads though; there's more ego, hope and sex drive than common sense in these creatures. Men see a lesbian as a beautiful challenge and a possible opportunity. They love the idea of a woman who will love other women, but hate that there may be a woman who doesn't consider his gender even remotely attractive.

Think about it from a guy's perspective; men see women as beautiful creatures - why shouldn't women be attracted to them as well? ...and it's just plain sexy!

MEN RESPOND TO VISUAL STIMULATION, WOMEN RESPOND MORE TO AUDITORY STIMULI.

This is pretty easy to deduce. Men look at women and get all hot and bothered. Men's eyes are constantly searching - many times against their will - for some visual stimulus they can latch onto. He looks for cleavage, braziers, panties, belly buttons... anything that he can see. This is where he gets most of his input on a situation anyway.

Women, on the other hand, are good listeners and this means that they rely much more on their hearing for stimulation. They want to hear a guy say that they love them... and need them. Women have this need to hear everything. The issue here is that men generally have problems with opening up and voicing their true feelings... they would rather just show them.

MEN AND WOMEN DO NOT RESPOND THE SAME TO TOUCH.

The concept of touch in a loving relationship is not where I'm going here. Lovers will many times respond to touch from their loved one in a positive way. But remember that men can fall in love with any female at anytime - so by contacting her with his body in any way, she has instantly become accessible; within reach so to speak. This is why men can sometimes respond to the touch of a woman so eagerly... she is so close!

Women don't usually respond in this way. Women don't just go out groping guys - even accidentally. Women are very protective of their emotions and bodies, and if an unwanted male invades that space, there can be dire consequences.

DON'T UNDERESTIMATE THE CUTE FACTOR.

There is an interesting relationship stabilizer that almost always helps, and we'll refer to it as the cute factor. This isn't solely based on looks; however, it is a component of it. The cute factor allows for a certain amount of forgiveness to be bestowed upon the cute party; basically because they are cute.

Cuteness is a combination of traits; looks, attitude, actions, outlook, and even a certain amount of naiveté or shyness are contributing factors. A relationship revolves around love, and we tend to love things that are cute.

If you think about it, it really does make sense. We don't want to see cute things suffer; we just want them to stay cute. So in the scheme of things, people will work harder in a relationship to bring joy to the cuteness. Just remember that different people have different ideas of what cute is.

While there are some people who find one sided devotion to be sad, others find it to be the epitome of cuteness; love against all odds and sense… it's naïve, but very cute.

A CERTAIN AMOUNT OF PERVERSION IS ACCEPTABLE.

I'm not talking about child molesting perversion, or twisted rapist perversion, but a more harmless perversion. This is pretty easy to understand, as most men are considered to be lecherous perverts anyway; but it's far more interesting when you come across a female with a little perverted streak in her... men would call that – a keeper.

There is nothing wrong with a little innuendo; nor having a 'healthy curiosity' about the physical characteristics of your relationship partner. Just remember that, in a relationship, your curiosity should be only explored with your partner; some actions invoke jealousy and anger in your mate.

THE SEXES

Men. Women. Boys. Girls. While there are great similarities in all people, there are also differences. This will compare and contrast the greatest battle of all... the best and worst in the battle of the sexes.

BEWARE OF THE FAIRIES.

I'm not talking about the little winged nymphs. I'm talking about the effeminate, cross dresser, fairy. There's a specific breed that I'm talking about here. Chances are this "female" is a musician, singer, actress, or artist... This is to hide the fact that inside is a martial artist, ninja, assassin, or otherwise dangerous character...

This seems to be more of an Asian custom, and is absolutely true. Bruce Lee was dressed as a girl in his youth to hide him from evil spirits; Jackie Chan played a female in numerous plays in his youth... these are some dangerous people here!

It's a trap! She may be hotter than the sun, and a talented artist/performer, but that's all part of the act... she's packing a sausage and probably 3 or 4 lethal weapons and the skills to destroy all of those who discover the ruse... BEWARE!

THE TOMBOY IS YOUR BEST FRIEND.

The tomboy female is probably more of a man than you are... She can fix vehicles, build battle armor, throw a good punch, and doesn't generally suffer from the same drawbacks as the girly girls. The tomboy is like a cool friend you can kiss. Oh, did I mention, this is not just the guys. Many times the tomboy is a female who can kiss either a boy or a girl, and no one will think less of her either way. This is one of the greatest evolutions of the female form; she can be bold, independent, self-sufficient, strong, and just as much a woman as the girly girls - just without all the maintenance.

The tomboy is a female who is sometimes difficult to get out of her shell, but if you can, you have a partner who will not just follow you anywhere, but she'll take the lead sometimes. She'll pick you up after a fall, she'll stay by your side... and she can fix your mech.

Don't invoke the wrath of the tomboy. She is your equal or better, and you will not have a fun time trying to get out of that predicament. You may be a dragon, but she's a tiger, and she can fend for herself. Don't speak down to her - she won't take your abuse.

THE GIRLY GIRL IS SO... LIKE... OH MY GOD!

Think valley girl, now add a little princess, maybe some leg warmers... and bang! The girly girl. This girl likes to get what she wants... she's pushy, arrogant, and has little regard for others' feelings. This is a relatively shallow personality; a lot of mouth but not a lot of brains. She generally has wild mood swings, is very emotional, and can be hurt... but she is vengeful. She is stubborn, high maintenance, and clingy.

This female has evolved as a type of prize for those in search of the woman they can get, without needing to have any depth of thought or personality to attain. As a matter of fact, the girly girl doesn't like complex thoughts, just happy fun joy joy!

Girly girls need love too, so you can get in there and give it the college try, but remember that you should probably be some form of athlete with an image complex – because birds of a feather flock together.

NICE GUYS ALWAYS FINISH LAST.
Some people are too nice for their own good. This pitiful excuse for a male is just that guy. He rolls over on command, hates confrontation, has self-confidence issues, cannot admit his own feelings, and is generally a pushover that everyone takes advantage of... or worse, abuses, because there is no fear of retribution.

This male has some redeeming qualities however. He is a good person; he's kind to everyone, helps old people, not abusive, and very resilient. He is confident that just by being himself, even with his flaws, people will eventually see him for the nice guy that he is, and he will be respected.

The good news is that this eventually happens most of the time... the bad news is that his high school years are going to suck.

Since he has issues admitting his own feelings to himself, he has an even harder time opening up to a girl. He generally is in such a state of confusion, that he is somewhat clumsy, uncomfortable, and hesitant in everything that he does.

This guy can be a great friend, and a loyal boyfriend... but good luck getting him... *he* doesn't even know what he wants. The girl of his dreams could corner him, grab his junk, rip off her clothes and jump him, and he would fight the whole way - or just faint with a nose bleed or something. He's a tough nut to get rolling, but for the woman who lands mister nice guy... it may be late... or even last, but there is no nicer guy.

THERE'S ALWAYS THE ONE GOOD GIRL.
Good girls get a few more bonus points than the good guys, but they have a little more risk in life. These genuinely good females

are naive to the ways of the world. They are nice to everybody. However, they are not generally shunned like the super nice guy. The main difference here is gender. Many of the same problems are inherent with being this type of person though.

There are usually similar issues with insecurity and self-consciousness, but this just seems like a coy, cute treat in a female; where with the guy it just seemed like he was somehow neutered. Like the guys, they are very aware that they are having feelings, even if they are having difficulty expressing them. This generally causes some similar side effects... blushing, fainting, hesitation, and self-confidence issues.

This girl runs a greater risk of being taken advantage of by the less scrupulous people in the world. Her naiveté can get her into trouble; she's usually too trusting. In her mind, all people are inherently good, and she deludes herself into thinking that she can change everyone with a little kindness and understanding. Big mistake.

The good news for this type of girl is that, if she is lucky she will get with a good person who will appreciate her kind heart; maybe mister nice guy?

BAD GIRLS CAN BE GOOD FOR YOU.

There's an interesting question related to the bad girls. Can bad girls be a good thing? Just like the ideas around universal balance, you must make an assumption that something can't be all bad. So continuing along those lines, let's look at the phenomenon of bad girls.

Bad girls are generally self-centered, manipulative, crass, powerful sociopaths. This is general, and this generality stretches from the high school hussy to the evil woman who can be damn close to demonic. How can this be a good thing? Let's look back at the good guys and good girls. Their negative traits are sometimes confidence, naiveté, or they're just far too trusting. How better to teach these good guys and gals that these traits are bad, than to have them taken advantage of?

The nice guy may have a crush on a bad girl who squashes their hopes; however, he had to build up the courage and confidence to ask in the first place. So, even though he may take a hit to his pride with the denial, he did actually advance forward. Life is a constant learning process and the bad girls are the teachers of what not to do.

Many times the bad girls are looking to absorb the happiness of others... so if a nice guy starts to make progress with a relationship, and the bad girl sees their happiness, she may try to kill the relationship by making advances on the nice guy. Well that's an interesting twist... this is a win-win situation when it comes to lessons... if he accepts the advances, his confidence is boosted, the girl who he was starting a relationship with learns to evaluate what the relationship meant to her. If it's worth fighting for, it may just give her the kick in the behind to start fighting for what's important to her. If she starts fighting, the guy now has two girls fighting for him - an even bigger boost!

If he denies the bad girl and stays steadfast with his resolve... he is confident with his decision, building him up because he has denied the advances. The girl he's with can be confident that he is true to her, and that builds confidence in the relationship. This is what bad girls are good for.

Bad girls can be good... however they can cause a bit of confusion and chaos depending upon their make-up... and I don't mean the stuff on their face. Some bad girls are truly heartless, evil wenches. This can teach tolerance and compassion, as well as the ability to "draw the line." You can tolerate nefarious activity for only so long, and because she's a female, people tend to give a little more slack. You still need the line though - the line that cannot be crossed.

The truly bad girl will brazenly cross this line... however many females have a mother complex somewhere in their genes that will kick in. Even bad girls can be cracked. There are exceptions to every rule of course, but the bad girls can be hurt too... chances are that they were hurt in the first place, initially triggering their bad attitude. If a bad girl was once good, and sees a good girl being abused the way she was, the bad girl may feel compassion for her. She may even get in there and do something good to help.

This may not make her a saint, but a little redemption is better than none.

MEN ARE PHYSICALLY STRONGER – USUALLY.

Due to forces beyond their control, women usually get the short end of the stick when it comes to physical strength. They however have a few tricks up their sleeves (or skirts) that can help them to overcome any foe, no matter how strong. This is a great equalizer, as most men just try to rely on superior strength to win any dispute. Women are not nearly so narrow-minded.

However, without running the risk of sounding too repetitive, we must remember that there are exceptions to every rule, and there are few exceptions that we collectively enjoy more than a strong woman. Strong women who can hold their own in a fight may be rare, but it's a beautiful thing when it happens. So come on ladies, give the guys a run for their money!

BIG FAT GUYS LOVE FOOD.

This may seem to be an obvious point, and it is. Fat guys can be big teddy bears, or vile monsters, but they all love food. Food is the great motivator for these calorie hounds. Having trouble moving a fat guy? Put food in the area you want him to go. The more food, the faster he gets there - Simple.

UNIVERSAL PERSONALITIES

CHAPTER 6

Now for a twist, there are some traits that transcend gender, and these just show how similar the sexes are... remember, we're all human... well for the most part.

YOU GOTTA LOVE THE FIGHTERS.

These are not bad people. They are generally good. Impulsive perhaps. Strong willed. Bold. These are the ones you can rely on when something is not going quite right. They will help you get through it. Got a bully problem? Here comes the fighter. The fighters understand that not everyone can act when it's needed... that's their job.

If you are a fighter, that's good for you. The big problem with fighters is that they are on that narrow line between good and bad. It just depends on who they're fighting for... or against. Fighters can have many enemies, but they also have lots of admirers. They are the ones you want to have on your team.

Some fighters are better adjusted than others. Some are cool headed, others fly off the handle. This trait doesn't really depend on gender either. Many of the most skilled fighter archetypes appear very subdued until action is required; then action is swift and effective... others are more like wild animals, attacking a situation with excessive force.

Fighters are great for morale, but can also be a crutch, generally being the ones who provoke a mob mentality. Fighters can be good politicians and tacticians; being used to trying to find the winning move. Fighters are not always helpful. Some situations call for a gentle hand, or undying patience; these are not the best ones to send a fighter into.

WELCOME TO THE VANITY FAIRGROUNDS!

There are always the people who love themselves more than anything else. They can't pass a mirror without looking at themselves. There's a definite ego here. These people can be humorous to watch. There are a few different ways to deal with these types. The easiest and most direct way is to find someone who is prettier than they are - especially if that other person is modest... it's like a slap in the face.

These people are more fun to mess with because they are so full of themselves, that they think everyone else thinks of them that way. These are image people - tarnish that image and BOOM! Instant fun!

These people have counterparts amazingly enough. It's just tough to get them to stop looking at themselves long enough to see them. It's difficult to get these people to care for anything other than themselves - play to their ego and it's possible - or just steal their mirror.

ANNOYING ATTENTION DEFICIT HYPERACTIVE PERSONALITIES ARE SEXLESS.

It would appear that there is always the hyper brat personality. This is a sad existence, mainly because most people would prefer they just go away. It's interesting to note that in the anime world, this is not generally a condition that requires medication. It does often include a little tough love and "redirection." This redirection could involve any number of interesting and creative methods; including humiliation, violence, over stimulation, or even the use of a pacifier. This concept should be evaluated for use in the real world.

It's also interesting to note that many of these hyper brats do not act this way all of the time, it almost seems targeted. If you are in the crosshairs, get creative... you'd be surprised. Mimicry is my personal favorite.

HERE'S TO THE LOSERS!

Not everyone can win. Some people just seem to always get the short end of the stick. These aren't the cool kids. These are the ones that never seem to catch a break; their biggest hopes are maybe sloppy seconds off a girl who has been dissed by one of the bad boys. It's easy to sympathize with the losers... everyone loses sometimes. You can relate to their plight; always wanting more, but concerned that if they stick their neck out, someone will cut their head off.

Losers come a in a few different varieties. You have the little, mousy, nerd ones. The big dumb oafs; and yes they come in male and female. The leery, creepy, losers are always around - and we can't forget the space cadets, drug addicts, mutants, emo-kids, and the down trodden.

It's interesting to realize that these people are what you would consider to be the majority. We're all losers in some way. Some have awkward little idiosyncrasies that make us stick out from time to time - sometimes in embarrassing ways. The good news for everyone is that when you get older, many of those traits become less noticeable, but that may only be for the reason that we are no longer under the microscope of school.

School turns most people into losers. There's always someone in that environment that thinks you're a loser... it just depends on who you are hanging around with at the time.

Jocks make fun of the band geeks and the brains. The brains feel that everyone is inferior. The popular people only like those who like them. So as you can see, everyone has a little bit of loser in them. Just some get the shorter end of the stick; the ones who are shunned by everyone.

The real losers in this environment huddle together more out of circumstance than out of any actual friendship reasons. They are just cast into the void and that's where they hook up. The good news is that there are people out there who pity them, respect them, and give them the benefit of the doubt. Even better news is that these people are the good boys and girls that you would really want to have as your friends anyway.

People find losers to be unthreatening, and therefore easy to break the ice with. Some of these so-called losers are really cool people - even if they are a little strange. You should not take the losers lightly though - they do have feelings, and if you think that some of them are a little strange, and you treat them that way - how do you think they deal with that?

They keep track... sort of a score card of who is not nice to them; those who shun them, taunt them, abuse them and humiliate them are always added to this list. This may not be an actual written list, however they are keeping track. Make amends. The losers are survivors, and once they have taken enough abuse they tend to lash out... this can be calculated or frenzied, either way, you don't want to be on that list.

So remember, we're all losers in some ways. *Here's to the losers!*

BEING FRIENDS

CHAPTER 7

We spend a lot of time in our lives with our friends. Friends are great resources, and contribute a lot to our development as people. Here are some random lessons about being friends.

FRIENDS MAKE FIERCE ENEMIES.

Because of the time you spend with your friends, and the amount you confide in them, they make powerful enemies. You have a person who knows everything about you - your habits, fears, loves, strengths, family, and most of all weaknesses. This is someone you want on your side. Now some of your friends are mischievous, and may seem like enemies because of how much they make your life difficult, but they are still friends. You definitely want to keep them that way.

A TRUE FRIEND WILL GIVE YOU EVERYTHING THEY HAVE AND EXPECT ONLY FRIENDSHIP IN RETURN.

In a materialistic world, it's difficult to find people who are still really good friends. Many people are greedy and look at other people with the assumption that they can get something out of them. But a true friend wishes only for friendship, companionship, and happiness from their dealings with you. They value you more than what they can get from you.

BEST FRIENDS GIVE THE BEST ADVICE.

Your friends know you very well. They see everything you go through, and they want you to be happy, because it makes them happy. They will give you advice from an outsider's view, while still knowing you well enough to help you with your goals. These friends will help you see the proper path, even when you are blinded to the fact that it's right in front of you.

MEN AND WOMEN MAKE DIFFICULT FRIENDS... UNLESS THEY ARE MOVING THE RELATIONSHIP TO ANOTHER LEVEL.

Guys generally have a tough time accepting most females as friends, and it isn't because they think that they are bad people, or wouldn't make good friends; guys get hung up on the fact that they are girls. It seems weird to admit that women can be completely platonic and men cannot, but the more I see it, the more I believe it. Even if men try to block the urges from their brains, they run the risk of being placed in a situation with a female, whom they are very comfortable with, that can make those thoughts difficult to overcome. This then causes difficulties with the friendship; especially if the guy wants to move forward and the girl just wants to be friends.

If they actually give in and allow passion to intervene, the friendship will never be the same; however, this can be good or bad. If they move the relationship to the next level, chances are it will be strong, considering the strong bond they already had as friends. This of course can backfire if they don't keep moving forward with the relationship; there can be awkwardness, resentment, anger, distrust, and more confusing feelings that will most likely doom the friendship, unfortunately.

Even if they force themselves to be platonic, the man will eventually move on, looking for a relationship with a female he can move forward with, because this is going nowhere – hence dooming the friendship in the end anyway; unless they are gay.

FRIENDS WANT TO HEAR YOUR PROBLEMS.

Good friends, male and female alike, are interested in helping their friends out. If there is something troubling their friend, they want to know what it is, to see if they can help fix it. Not only can they help, but they can tell *when* you have a problem. Your friends can be very close to you, and they see you when you're happy, sad, angry, annoyed, frustrated, and sometimes just melancholy; they know when something is wrong. Women are generally better at this than men, due to their inherent empathy for others, but when a guy is around their friend all the time, they know when to ask, "What's wrong with you?"

The biggest difference between men and women is that women will talk about their emotions and feelings to their friends, more readily than men will. This is a self-delusion by men that, by having emotions, they may seem weak. It's not in a guy's nature to ask for help with feelings. Women on the other hand, seem to get more emotional reinforcement from their friends, and readily speak about their problems with their good friends.

A FRIEND WILL TAKE ONE FOR THE TEAM.

There is a certain amount of noble self-sacrifice that comes into play when talking about friends. Think of the number of times you have taken the heat for one of your friends. Maybe you've covered for them, lied for them, or spoke to someone that they were fond of for them; we do a lot for our friends.

Friends like to take action for their friends; they don't just like sitting around watching their friend's lives. People like to feel important, and how better to do that than to help out your friend? Sometimes you need to take the heat, or make a sacrifice. Perhaps you need to do something that you would rather not do, but action is required (i.e. you get the ugly girl.) Sometimes the best action we can take as friends is to just jump in there and take one for the team.

AS WE GROW OLDER OUR FRIENDS BECOME LESS IMPORTANT.

When we are young, friends play an important part in our lives, but there comes a time when you need to break off from that safety and venture out on your own. Friends help us grow as people, and initially we need a lot of help; we don't even know what we want. Our friends help us to build our base set of values and help us to define who we are and what we want. However, when we get older, we no longer need outside influence to decide what we want. This is when we move on from those relationships, to explore our own paths in the best way that we know how; relying upon ourselves. The early development we went through with our friends is our greatest weapon.

When you leave school, life becomes a more personal journey - this isn't to say we don't still have friends, but after a while they aren't as important. In the end, we live for ourselves, and what makes us happy - and we can only really explore that on our own.

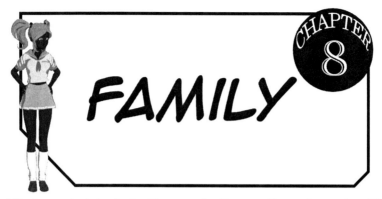

FAMILY

The joys and trials of a family can make life rewarding or devastating. You are brought into this world, unaware of anything - and that which we call family, is there waiting for you.

EVERYONE'S FAMILY IS DIFFERENT.

There are families that are large, small, new, old, married, divorced, happy, and unhappy. It's impossible to cover all the variations of families, but remember that no two are the same. Sure there might be an outward appearance of a family that seems average, but since every person is different, so then is every family. A family with troubles may be the happiest family on the block; where the wealthy family may have a distant and tortured attitude toward the rest of their family members. Families can build a person up, by being supportive and caring, or drag them down with ridicule and abuse.

YOU CAN'T CHOOSE YOUR FAMILY.

The one thing we have no control over in this world is what family we will be born into. This fact makes the concept of family almost strange to talk about. Why would you discuss that which you cannot change? Well, even though you cannot choose your family, there are ways that you can make it better. You may have stubborn siblings, overbearing parents, crazy cousins, evil step sisters, dopey step brothers, and more... but this isn't the end of the world. This is another part of life. You need to play with the hand you've been dealt.

Some people were brought up in unhealthy families, but they overcame that situation and went on to become very successful and well-mannered. How is that possible? Well, life has a funny way of testing our resolve; the one thing you cannot escape is your birth. After that, it's up to you. Some people depend on friends, others have extended family, others still are orphans, but they get along... as will you. Your ability to deal with any situation, including a rough upbringing, is what our characters are built from.

DON'T TAKE YOUR FAMILY FOR GRANTED.

If you happen to be fortunate enough to have a family, especially a close one, don't take them for granted. The family bonds run deep, and are difficult to break, but that doesn't mean that you should take them for granted. You family will always be a part of you, and that bond is stronger than any friendship; you can lose a friend in a fight, but your family is still your family. Why turn that against you?

Everyone has some form of issue with their family; this is natural. The main reason this occurs is because you don't get to choose them. You can choose your friends and have them for life... but *you* choose them. The difference is that you can choose to treat your family well, or not. The choice is up to you, and choose wisely; families can be vengeful, and remember that they are bound to you - forever.

EVERY BOY IS A MAMA'S BOY.

Being the first large female influence in a boy's life, a mother has a great deal to do with a boy's expectations of females in the future. There is always strength to a mother, even if she seems timid; she is the homemaker. This helps define what a male should be looking for in a girl. Kind, loving, unconditional respect, but still a teacher and maybe even a slight disciplinarian;

men seek out these attributes in the ones they choose as their mates. Men are attracted to women who have some of the attributes of their mothers, because these attributes are the ones they grew up loving and respecting as feminine.

EVERY GIRL IS A DADDY'S GIRL.

This is a slightly different perspective than the mama's boy. The girls grow up with a father who is similar to them in the way the mother is to the son, but the girls get a completely different image. They learn to love the strength of the father, if not all of his traits. Men do tend to fuss over their daughters though. This gives girls their first impressions of how a man is supposed to be - the provider, disciplinarian, the protector, and the attention giver. As with the men, this is more of a set of characteristics, than an actual person.

The girls are protected by their fathers and loved... but if the home life is bad, this can have a devastating effect on the young girl's image of what a good man is. Many women who choose abusive husbands had abusive families before, and this cycle continues.

BOYS LEARN HOW TO ACT FROM THEIR FATHERS.

As much as the growing lad adores his mother, he also looks to latch onto a father figure to emulate. This can be a good thing or a bad thing. If the father is kind and good, this is generally a good thing. If the father is completely absent, then the boys will find another. This can lead to a whole bunch of issues in the male development. The good news is that this can be overcome with a strong will, character, and the urge to do the right thing. There are things that help people - good things... and there are things that hurt people - those are bad. If the male grows up in a household where the father is gone, or worse... it will then be up to the character of the boy himself.

GIRLS LEARN HOW TO GET GUYS FROM THEIR MOM.

Now, it may be easy to say that girls learn more from their friends and in school than they do from their mothers. Well this is possible in the broad context of life, but the basics are still taught by mom. A mother can teach a daughter a great many things about getting a guy. Be kind, caring and responsible. Learn to cook and clean and care for your man and family.

SIBLINGS CAN BE A PAIN.

It's good to realize that siblings are in the same boat as you; constantly seeking attention and love, the same as you. However, this sometimes does not make it any easier to accept their behavior. Sometimes you have to deal with a sibling who just doesn't care at all for their other siblings. They can be a pain, but not nearly as bad as going into a jealous rampage over the attentions of the rest of the family, or friends. This can be an uneasy rivalry, because it's difficult to escape the reach of someone who is so close to you.

This has a flip side though. Sometimes all that you have in life is a sibling. Maybe you are timid, or confused about life, and you have a sibling who is there for you. Even though they can be a pain, many times this rivalry can be overcome in times of crisis or difficulty. In this case siblings can be the most reliable resource you have... they know you, and your needs... and they are still family.

CHAPTER 9

SCHOOL

While we are going through school, we are going through a very important period of adjustment. When we start school, we are unable to care for ourselves, and by the time we leave, we are expected to be fully functioning adults; being completely self-supporting. This time is full of chaos; where all of the lessons we need to learn are not just taught to us by our teachers, but we learn from others as well.

HAVE A CRUSH ON ONE OF YOUR TEACHERS.

There's nothing wrong with a healthy crush on one of your teachers. This can help you to understand a few simple lessons in itself. It's probable that this crush is a passing fancy, and is completely unattainable, but it teaches you to feel for those who are trying to help you. It also teaches you that not every emotion and feeling you have can or should be acted upon.

You may also find that you do better in the class of the teacher you have a crush on. This is because you are trying your best for them; also an important lesson. You try hardest for the ones you love - even if this love is unattainable.

OBSERVE YOUR LIKES AND DISLIKES.

School is a time when we are developing, so it's good to be an observer. You should pay attention to the things that interest you; the people, subjects, lessons, activities, and environments that you are enthralled by, and those that are distasteful to you. School is a long road with a lot of lessons, but the main lesson is to help you find you; and to help you to live the rest of your days, outside of school, with dignity, compassion, enthusiasm, and morality. How can you start to learn these things unless you first observe them?

TAKE YOUR PUNISHMENT, YOU EARNED IT.

If you do something wrong in school, many times you will be punished - if you are caught that is - and if you do indeed deserve it... accept it. The lesson here is that there are consequences for your actions. You must learn this as early as possible, unless you really like being punished. This can be a double edged sword though. Here's an example...

If you have a crush on a teacher, and find you can't get their attention by doing well, then you may revert to the dark side; trying to get their attention through malice. This isn't the best approach to a situation. Just remember that this is someone you like, and you are making their life more difficult by acting that way... and that isn't the way we treat the ones we love.

EVERYONE IS DIFFERENT, BUT WE ARE ALL THE SAME.

School is usually the first place we run into great diversity. Which is why it's such a great place to learn about it; different gender, races, age, weight, social status, intelligence, and beauty are all things we learn about in school. Some of these lessons are easy, and some are hard. Try to learn these lessons with a certain curiosity and compassion - this will make it so you don't just jump to conclusions and hurt someone. People are all different, but we are all the same. The one who is superior is the one that recognizes this, and remembers that no one is to be taken for granted, no feelings are to be taken lightly, and no one is made better by putting yourself over someone else; but it is by supporting others that you become greater.

LEARN AS MUCH AS YOU CAN ABOUT EVERYTHING.

No one can learn everything, but as people we tend miss the importance of things we don't understand. If a person is misunderstood, we may not see them as very important. But you don't know for sure, because you don't understand them. It is important to try to learn things, and understand them yourself - don't just take someone's word for it. The more you learn, the more you can find out for yourself what is important, and what is not.

There's a side effect to this, the more you know, the more you're needed. While you're in school, everyone around you is going through the same process; wake up, get breakfast, go to school, hang out with friends, learn more stuff... etc. So the more you take advantage of the little opportunities you have to learn, the better off you'll be. People will need you because they didn't pay attention to the value of learning at every moment.

THE BEST WAY TO UNDERSTAND SOMETHING IS TO TEACH IT.

Learning things in your own way, for yourself, can be difficult at times; but trying to teach someone something is all that much more challenging and rewarding. It's easy to see things from your own point of view; we do it all the time. Everyone doesn't think like you or learns the same way that you do - so you must adapt. You need to understand the material in more than one way, to be able to apply it in a different way so that someone else can learn it. It's not easy to do... but it does help you learn something better.

The main reason for this is that you have to look at something many different ways - an important skill in itself. But by seeing it from all of those different angles, you can get a more complete picture of what something really is; hence learning it better through teaching.

SOME OF YOUR TEACHERS MAY ACTUALLY BE PRETTY COOL.

Many people go through school thinking that their teachers are a separate species or something - all strict and no personality. It is possible that you are just not giving them a chance. Now granted, they are there for a reason, to teach you, but you may not be asking the right questions to get the lesson you want. Your teachers are people, just like you; they were young, just like you. Teachers have a lot to teach, not just about academics, but about life. Also remember that many teachers are there to learn. There's a certain side effect to working with younger people all the time, some of the youth rubs off on you - and many teachers aren't afraid to admit that they are learning as much about life by teaching you, as you are learning from them.

ENJOY YOUR SCHOOL TIME.

This is the only real time in your life dedicated to learning everything about everything. This is a time for learning and discovery - not only about the world, but about your self. You may have chores and studies, and these may seem like work - being tedious and seemingly taking forever. However, it is good to remember that this is the time in your life where time seems to stand still, and seconds can seem like minutes. What you don't understand is that time will not always travel this slowly, and when you get older, time travels faster, to where a day can be as a minute...

Enjoy your time in school. There is so much life and learning that you can cram into a day - more than some grownups do in a year.

AGING

As we age, we face a great deal of changes - starting at birth and going until we die. You can learn a lot from looking at the process of aging and the lessons to be learned at each stage.

CHILDREN ARE THE FUTURE.

This is true however you look at it. If you nurture the youth, then you will protect the future. If you neglect the children, then you leave the future in a state of neglect. The future is a big enough unknown without leaving it to the hands of fate. Children need to be educated, tolerant, respectful, and adaptive - they will learn the other skills later in life.

TEENAGERS' LIVES SUCK.

Teenagers have a tough existence. Their bodies are changing; they are raging hormone factories. They are under close watch from their elders, and are in constant struggle between obedience and independence. Teens are learning the skills they will need for the future, but they are not in a position to freely use these skills. This is a rough time for people.

There is always a struggle; struggle with self-image, friends, sexuality, independence, individuality, and their own future. Teens always feel like they know everything or nothing; that they are worshipped or ignored - the extremes of thought. They feel either loved or hated. This is a time of powerful emotions and change.

Teens live and love with more of their being... they hate with all their heart and love with all their soul. They are fragile and indestructible at the same time. This is a time when the decisions that they make will shape their character for the rest of their lives.

Trauma during this stage of development can be catastrophic - and trauma comes easy to the teens. Teens are subject to conditions that leave them exposed to everything. They are very dependent upon friends, fall in and out of love, and embarrassment and rejection are fates worse than death.

Teens are hypersensitive to those around them, especially in times of strife. They are stubborn, selfish, envious, and cruel... They are also very aware that those surrounding them are capable of the same. This is when you see the individuals clashing within groups, as some will claw their way to the top by being perceived as better... others will be stomped on, as their individual traits may seem useless to the others.

EARLY ADULTHOOD BRINGS THE NEED TO ACCEPT RESPONSIBILITY.

After being allowed to run amok for the first 18 to 20 years of life, with few responsibilities, young adulthood brings a time when the physical development slows, and the character cements itself into the psyche. This is where teenagers become adults... they have to take responsibility for their own futures. They must start to consider the issues of family, survival, mortality, self-control, and responsibility for more than just their own feelings.

This is a time when the adversities they encountered during their teens are sorted through, evaluated, and filed; this is where the adult begins. It is a time of big questions. This is when they discover what is important, what it really means to be responsible, and what love and hate really are - as well as how they will play their role in the future.

If the teenagers went through a normal development to this point, then you will have reasonably well-rounded young adults, who are tolerant, compassionate and responsible. If the process of development was chaotic or extreme, then you get adults who exhibit extreme behavior... like teens with amplified resolve.

This time can be difficult for those who were really dependent upon others during their teen years. They may go through feelings of abandonment and loneliness, as those they relied upon become independent and move on. People become somewhat less selfish and more serving at this point... serving the ideals that they have deemed worthy.

MIDDLE AGE... AUTOPILOT TIME.

This is generally a time when life has settled. You are willing to accept compromise for stability, and you spend increasing time reflecting on the past, accumulating wisdom, pondering the future, and reevaluating the choices that you made during your early years.

This is a great time to give back to the younger generations who may not appreciate you now, but will appreciate you later for your guidance. This is the time when you start to appreciate what you have, what you've lost, and those who have helped you along the way. You reach a point where you have ambition that isn't for you, but for the future.

If you have a family, it is growing up faster than you can imagine. You are still understanding of youthful problems, but they are somewhat foreign in their manifestations. You are a different generation now, and you begin to find yourself further distancing yourself from the youth and teens. You are a true adult now. You have many responsibilities, and you are constantly preoccupied with them.

Time flies during this stage of your life... hours, days weeks, months, years, and decades... You have so much to do, that has to get done, that you have less time for what you want - but this is the path you've chosen. It gets harder to accept change. You are more concerned with safety, mortality, and defending the choices you've made in life... as if trying to prove to yourself that you have done everything you wanted... but you have really only done what you needed to do.

ENTERING THE WANING YEARS.

After a couple decades of autopilot, you have become somewhat bitter; you are watching your children's children grow up now. You are beginning to realize how out of touch you are with the world and the youth of today. You can sympathize more with the middle aged people, who are constantly sacrificing what they want to do for what they need to do. You are becoming more like a young adult, concerning yourself with the future, but for different reasons.

You are in the position to give the future generations the wisdom and leadership to become responsible adults, and do what they need to do. You are still somewhat brazen; passing responsibility onto the future generations as you begin to confront your own death head on. You may not have come to accept your own mortality yet, but you understand that nothing is infinite.

You pass your ideals onto the youth, having forgotten that they are so preoccupied with life that they have little time for your abstract wisdom... they have "real" problems.

ELDERS ARE THE NEW TEENS.

You begin to act out in order to recapture some of the youth you sacrificed to do what you needed to do... now you start living for yourself. You have accepted that you are going to die, and with that acceptance comes a sort of brazen act of defiance. You know that you are not indestructible, but you understand that it's only a matter of time anyway... so live it up. You don't care what people think anymore; you can even be a dirty old man, and people will humor you...

Where the teens didn't consider death in their actions, you are finished worrying about it. This turns you into a teen again. You become very interested in people's personal lives. Maybe you get a new lease on life... a renewed sense of spirit and fun. You know that you can do whatever you want, so you do.

You have accepted that every generation has its own issues, and they all need to take responsibility for those issues. This is no longer your problem as you are more concerned with your wants... maybe you want to give wisdom... maybe you want to skydive... who knows? You are your own person now, and you answer only to yourself...

You have little to learn these days, and you become more of an observer; watching all of the life around you. You also become more of an encyclopedia of lessons in life, and you can accept your fate with dignity - but you may just be shrinking and becoming a pervert again.

HANGING ONTO THE END OF THE THREAD OF LIFE.

Eventually everyone needs to go. In the end, if you were fortunate enough to live out a full life, you become as you were in the beginning – a dependant. There are a few big differences. The baby had no regret, the toddler had no wisdom, the teen didn't understand mortality... and now you are going to take the step which no one will return from... the great unknown.

You are still a valued person, and you may find that people come to speak with you just because they want your wisdom on life... but many of the lessons that you have to teach are about how to be graceful in the end, and how to live life to the fullest, because it will end for everyone. You have your regrets and you learn to accept them. You make it a point to tell everyone that wisdom is everything... maybe because it's all you have left... and you can't just let it go...

No matter how wise a person is, we all face death knowing nothing.

AGING IS ACCEPTING THE INEVITABLE.

In order to truly grow up, and progress through life, we must accept that this process is happening. It is easy to see the truth in this. If you are wise enough to pay attention, you will see the youngsters that think they are invincible having problems with growing up; where those who have faced hardship and death, and have accepted it, are generally more mature.

There's nothing wrong with being jaded about aging – we all do it to some degree, but we still need to remember to live our lives. If we fool ourselves into thinking that we will never age and die, we will forget to live life like it can end at any time. This knowledge can be disturbing to some; but to others it helps them live every day to the fullest – because they are alive now, and they are going to live it up!

Many of the standards set forth by society are visible in anime. Many cultures have their own social norms, customs, fashions, or acceptable behaviors... it's interesting to see how they overlap.

SCHOOL GIRLS IN UNIFORM ARE HOT.

I don't know who came up with these school uniforms for the girls, but it seems to be a global conspiracy. Uniforms do vary in a few areas but the standards are pretty much the same. There's something to be said about a school that dresses their girls up in a way that accentuates the female form. I don't know who came up with it, but it's brilliant. I can see how it helps with the male attendance.

GIRLS LIKE GUYS IN UNIFORM.

If you have to dress up in a uniform and you are a guy, then you are probably running the risk of either looking like a young republican, or some unknown branch of the military. This could be good or bad. I guess in certain environments, girls like a guy in uniform.

BEAUTY IS A HIGHLY PRAISED TRAIT.

It's an interesting paradox that you are told to look past one's physical features to truly appreciate them, yet it's our first indication that someone is desirable. Brains are not the number one trait that it considered. People have this need to praise beauty, whether it is clothes, jewelry, makeup, or just physical attributes - we praise the pretty.

It would appear this is somewhat universal, even if the views of beauty are different; it has the same value in a society. Beauty is in the eyes of the beholder, and everyone has different views, but beauty is, in essence, the Holy Grail.

INTELLIGENCE IS ALSO HIGHLY PRAISED, BUT USUALLY IN MODERATION.

There's something cold and unappealing about a robot, and there are some people who have almost computer-like brains. If that's all they are - all brains, no personality, no sense of humor, no other redeeming qualities - then they're useful, but they're boring! What's the point of having a brain and no character?

A CERTAIN AMOUNT OF CHAOS IS NOT ONLY ACCEPTABLE, IT'S REQUIRED.

In society there are some things that exist in an almost sterile state; completely organized and right. This isn't really the way things should be. Chaos is a part of everyday life. It keeps us alert and evaluating new possibilities. Without chaos there would be no adventure or invention. There would be no nervousness, or doubt. There would be no fear, and there would be no love. How can you live in a world where everything appears to be predetermined - a place where there's no possibility of accidental situations or wardrobe malfunctions?

Perfect order in society is not an option. Many of the reasons why we have social norms in the first place are to regulate chaos. Why do you think we have laws and rules? If there was no chaos, there would be no reason for all those rules. No reason for government, laws, borders, weapons, pizza joints, short skirts, weightlifting, dating, courtship, work or marriage. What fun would life be?

Chaos is a good thing, in general. We are not in control of anything anyway if you think about it, but the illusion of control helps people to stay sane. The chaos is always present though.

NOTHING IS MORE MISUNDERSTOOD THAN BALANCE.

There is this idea that everyone understands balance in the universe. Society has this belief as well; however, the truth is that no one really seems to get it. There are those who have nothing; no food, shelter, love, family, friends, power, or money - and others who have an excess of it. Balance doesn't mean what a lot of people think it means. Balance, in the true sense, should mean that for every action there is an equal and opposite occurrence.

This isn't always plain to see, and this is where the misunderstanding comes into force. Everyone tries to find the balance, but it's not always something to be seen. This puts everyone in a state of trying to prove the truth and balance in everything; and gives us all our little hopeful comments like, "*everything happens for a reason*" and "*every cloud has a silver lining.*" Some things just happen and there's no other reason than, "*that's just the way it is.*"

SOCIETY NEEDS VARIOUS OTHER CULTURES.

Life would be boring without variety, and there's only so much variety you can get from your own culture. It would appear that many societies have begun to reach out to other cultures for influence. If your culture has no explanation for a certain phenomenon, why not look elsewhere?

People enjoy experiencing the things that will broaden their minds. People don't just watch a single movie over and over, nor do they watch a single genre of movie over and over. Certainly there are phases that people go through, but in general, we enjoy varied cultural influences. How else would culture evolve, other than having an outside influence?

Cultures that restrict access to outside influences are stagnant and do not possess the resources and insight needed to grow. All societies are different, because all people are different; and to leave this vast pool of culture untapped, is to invite stagnation and eventual destruction.

It is true that some cultures clash. There are societies that place emphasis on tradition and ritual, where others promote change and revolution. It's difficult to see one existing without the other, but it's the ones that embrace all the ideals that evolve the fastest, and with the most effectiveness.

SYMBOLS ARE IMPORTANT.

Different social groups, cultures, religious groups, clubs, and throngs of people have different symbols that they assign various meanings and value to. These symbols don't need to be ornate to be important. A person could be a symbol, or it can be written, scribed, embroidered, painted or even tattooed. People are very good at assigning value to symbols. We can use them as idols or just to differentiate between sub groups in the society. Think of all the symbols we have; the different flags, crests, religious symbols, corporate logos, military ranks, branches, government agencies, and institutions. Take due notice of different symbols and govern yourself accordingly; it may save your goose.

POWER

CHAPTER 12

There are few things in the world more sought after than power; whether it's money, status, influence or strength. Power is one of the few searches that, if you succeed, you can cause more suffering than if you failed. It's impossible to cover all the manifestations of power, but here are some important lessons...

ALL POWERFUL THINGS MUST HAVE A SEAL.

It would appear that powerful things just can't be trusted. You have to contain them somehow; either limiting their accessibility, use, or even limiting their power output; these powerful things must be sealed. This seal is usually proportionate in complexity to the power of that which it seals. This generally means the difference between a seal similar to the wax seals used to keep people from tampering with documents, to the 4th dimensional Rubik's cube, which can be used to seal the demons away in a place where they will float helpless for all eternity.

This is present in the real world as well. There are child proof lids on prescription drugs, biometric safes for handguns, as well as the monster security systems and forces protecting the world's nuclear arsenals. If it has power, it has a lock, key, security force, and a 4th dimensional Rubik's cube, that can only be defeated by beating it the day before you bought it.

POWER CORRUPTS, AND ABSOLUTE POWER CORRUPTS...UH...MORE.

Once the power is revealed, even the most caring can be tempted to abuse this power for personal and selfish endeavors. Sure you can save the world with lots of work and pain - but you can also use that power to live comfortably for the rest of eternity, if you play your cards right. Power makes people do strange things; you can destroy your whole family, tribe, community, city, continent, planet, solar system, or even universe... but it always seems that this is some display to get people to worship you. It just seems that people want to use power to get what they want, not what is right for the greater good.

UNIVERSAL POWER BALANCE MUST BE MAINTAINED.

There always seems to be a universal force or power in everything. It's a sort of balance that needs to be maintained. Power cannot be created or destroyed, merely changed from one form to another, or transferred from one being to another. This power can be a fuel, life force, magic, or technology. This universal truth about power cannot be thrown out of balance, no matter how hard you try.

You can try to wish it away, obliterate it, hurl it into the cosmos, or lock it away (with a cool seal perhaps!), but the balance will always equalize. Maybe things are better for the short term, or maybe they are worse. Maybe the entire population of your planet has been wiped out... somewhere out there balance is maintained.

This is one of the more difficult rules to believe in, and one of the easiest to assume that there are exceptions for. The only people who believe in exceptions to this are generally doing it for selfish reasons; corrupted by power, trampled on, or just seemingly cursed by fate, they assume that there is no balance. This is apparently just people forgetting that the world is bigger than they are, and the universe doesn't really care *when* your girlfriend/wife/vehicle explodes, leaving you alone to fend for yourself.

PACIFISTS ARE JUST AS BAD AS WARMONGERS... IF NOT WORSE.

Sure, you may think that the tree-hugging pacifists are great. All they want to do is live in peace. All they want is to not be bothered or confronted by anyone. All they want is everything to be nice and happy, and to force all of those warlike people to stop fighting and bend to their will. They want the power to control thought and action... They are power hungry. Carry a weapon into a town of pacifists, and see how quickly you are attacked. They always have a double standard, and this double standard throws off the balance of force... this almost always causes war and pain.

If your society hates anything... even if you hate violence, you are still hating, and hate is not love - But you can't love everything either. Pacifists say that they want to live in peace with all things... this is a lie. They want to live in peace with all things peaceful, just like them; reveling in their high and mighty peace train, damning all others to exile or destruction.

The ironic part is that once the peace-loving hippies snap, and rage into battle, they are some of the most brutal warriors - enraged by the thought that their ideal has been shattered and everything must now be destroyed.

BE WARY OF THE POWER OF ANY GOVERNMENT.

One of the functions of any government is to maintain and regulate order and power. They have the power to help, harm, save, or destroy. It's an interesting situation; having the power to control so many, with so few. This power can easily be abused.

Many governments try to show a benevolent face of brotherhood and peace, while stabbing their swords into other people's lives. Other governments don't hide their deeds and rule through the fear of retribution. The point is that the masses allow this power to go unchecked in many cases. We sometimes turn a blind eye to the problem and hope that it is all done in our best interests.

As people under the rule of a government, we have the responsibility to question and regulate the actions of our rulers; for if this power goes unchecked and unregulated, it can be abused in ways that may be detrimental to everyone. Our governments have the power to declare and wage war, suppress revolution, and remove the rights of its citizens… this is a power that, without regulation, can cause hardships for all – watch them with due diligence.

CRIME & CRIMINALS

There are a lot of immoral decisions that get made in the universe. Many times we chock this up to bad people doing bad things - sometimes to good people. This isn't always the case, as there are many different reasons people commit these acts. There's a lot of grey area, and while there are some cut and dry crimes and criminals, many are not that way.

NOT ALL CRIME IS TREATED THE SAME, EVEN IN THE MIND.

As humans we tend to rate crimes on a scale of evil. It's how we make decisions. Some people's scales are a little strange; either by necessity, situation, or group mentality. Sometimes people, who would never commit a crime, find reasons to make it acceptable. A starving child can steal food, a poor man can commit fraud, and a group of junkies can rob a drug dealer to get their fix. All of these are crimes of theft, but for some reason we don't look at the starving child in the same way as a group of junkies.

It would appear that the crime of stealing food is ok if you are starving, but drugs are wrong, so anyone stealing, using or selling them is instantly vilified. There are other crimes that have a similar stigma. Killing is wrong, and there are not a lot of good reasons for doing it, so it's a very tough one to try to explain, if it ever happens. It's also a tough one to have to live with.

THE GROPER MAY JUST BE A REAL CLUMSY GUY.

We tend to be overly harsh against anyone who invades our personal space, comfort zone, or privacy. Most guys have at some point in their lives been caught in the act of mentally undressing a pretty girl. This can sometimes cause panic, which is never a good way to try to fix the problem. Panic and stress cloud people's minds and motor skills. If this were to occur on a crowded subway or some other situation, it may be possible to make a fool out of yourself. Maybe losing your balance and falling, and if you're unlucky, landing with some part of your body on top, under, or in between some very inappropriate places. This causes more panic, making the situation worse, and now everyone thinks that the guy who had the wandering eyes is a lecherous pervert.

Now I'm not saying there aren't people out there who are lecherous gropers, but this isn't always the case. Granted that some people have a better sense of balance, timing, and self control, but the hormonal teenager is generally not this person. Many guys go through an awkward stage in life with females; it doesn't necessarily make them criminals.

THERE ARE SOME REAL BAD CRIMES AND SOME REAL BAD CRIMINALS.

Some criminals are really bad people; obtaining pleasure from the pain of others. There are indeed malicious people out there in the world, and you never know when they are going to happen by. There is no good way of anticipating when they are going to strike. Some are cold, calculating killers, others are opportunistic, and a few are just crazed loonies. In the fractured morality of these criminals, their crimes may become an obsession, where they are compelled to commit them.

How can you tell the difference? Sometimes it's hard to do. Some people may have inner demons that torment them and drive them to do bad things. Others evolve into this state. They can be anyone... and that's the scariest part - you never know.

66

MANY TIMES THE CRIMINAL BECOMES A VICTIM.

People tend to think that the ones who commit crimes are somehow inhuman, but it's good to remember that anyone can be driven to do these things. In the right situation, with enough strain, anyone can crack. Let's revisit the clumsy groper. Maybe he does trip and fall and grab a girl inappropriately, then in the process of trying to explain his position, and how he's sorry, he is assaulted - either by the victim or by those around. At this point a clumsy person is being assaulted; he has become the victim, for something he couldn't control.

Some of these people have become violent due to their distaste about this chain of events that, though unfortunate, were not malicious. This situation places the malice on the aggressors, not the klutz – he's just uncoordinated.

SOME CRIMES ARE ACCIDENTS.

The concept of an accidental crime seems foolish; if it was an accident, then it should not be a crime. There's a fine line between an accident and a reckless action. There are always people who act before they think, indeed most people have done this from time to time. This could be considered reckless, however it doesn't necessarily mean criminal. If you make an honest mistake, like picking up the wrong bag and walking away, because you thought it was yours, is that a crime? There are some that would say, "you stole it."

It's a strange world where crime is often determined by perception, and even a seemingly innocent mistake can be construed as a malicious crime.

ANYONE CAN BE THE CRIMINAL.

Especially in a mystery with few clues, there's no way of knowing who the person is that committed the crime. In this case, you may become so preoccupied with the crime, collection of clues, and search for a motive or alibi, that you forget to keep your eyes open for the unknown. It's possible that the criminal is right in front of your eyes - or may even be yourself.

Maybe that object wasn't stolen, it was misplaced. Maybe you lost it? Who knows? But the point is that you may be so busy accusing people of doing it, that you forget to check your other jacket, pants, bag, or even just your other pocket before jumping to conclusions.

GOOD & EVIL

CHAPTER 14

Sometimes good and evil can be easily determined, but most of the time in life, as in anime, it is more complicated than that. Sometimes it's a fine line, marked clearly, other times it's a nebulous grey area, when you may not know which side of the line you are on. Things are not always what they appear.

GOOD GIRLS GET HURT, BAD GIRLS HAVE MORE FUN.

Let's just be honest... all girls wish, at some point in their lives, to be one of the bad girls. It's easier to pretend that having no morals will mean that you will suffer no pain. This is the allure of being one of the bad girls. You can do whatever you want, to whoever you want, and not worry about anything. You can control your destiny and rely upon impulses to govern your actions... but the good girls always seem to get the short end of the stick.

They get stepped on, used, manipulated, they are far too trusting, and always trying to delude themselves into a sense of "if I do good things, good things will happen to me." All the while, the good girls are watching the bad girls do whatever they want and get whatever they want.

As I said before, this can be a grey area. A good girl can dismiss a situation as harmless, doing more harm than good; and a bad girl can do something selfish that turns out to be a beneficial course of action. In life, many times, good and bad are a matter of circumstance.

THERE IS SUCH A THING AS OVERKILL.

You can over-do anything. You may have a task to do that seems like a good thing, and you spend so much time and effort thinking about how best accomplish it, that you don't see the forest for the trees. Then by the time you realize it, you have overdone it; you were trying to protect someone and you ended up imprisoning them, or worse, destroying them. You can smother anything if you try hard enough; you can drown someone in affection, kill someone with compassion, and you can beat someone down while trying to raise their spirits.

On the flipside, you can also go too far on the side of evil. You can work so hard to destroy something which you perceive as a threat, that you fail to realize that you needed it. You can be the parasite that kills the host and then dies a slow death from your greed. You can exterminate all of your obstacles to attain the prize and take all the pleasure out of the victory, because there is nothing more to gain.

WHICH IS WORSE – BEING KILLED BY FAMILY, FRIENDS, OR A LOVER?

There are few questions more complicated than this. Which is more evil; to be killed as a direct result of the actions of a friend, family member or a lover? As in life, there are no good answers to this question. The situation and intentions govern the answers.

It becomes more complicated when you add a mix of the three. Is it ok to allow a friend to kill a family member to save a lover? What if it's not a friend? What if the family member was old and you didn't like them much anyway? What if the person you loved didn't love you back? Can you sacrifice a loved one to save your family? Can you allow a person that you love to sacrifice themselves to save you? Can you sacrifice yourself to save a loved one?

It is difficult to define a "good versus evil" argument here, but these are the grey areas... where do you draw the line? These are some of the questions that make these stories so compelling. They allow us to see different situations handled different ways, with different results. Something that seems right, may be very wrong...

...and what happens when the choice isn't up to you?

If you were killed by a family member who was coveting your love interest, that would be evil... correct? Well, what if you were the overbearing one in the relationship, and they were in love without your knowledge?

Is killing your enemy's lover justified? Does it make you evil to do that? Can you justify it if they are a non-combatant?

WHAT IS RIGHT DEPENDS ON WHICH SIDE YOU ARE ON.

You may think that your enemy is a heartless infidel. You may think that they are evil. You may believe that all their ideals are wrong. However, that is the view from your side... what do you think you look like to them?

It is difficult to define right and wrong, or good and evil, from the standpoint of a single person at a single point in time. What would happen if Hitler won WWII? Wouldn't he be the hero? A revolt or insurrection is only considered bad by those who are in power, or in support of that power. If the American Revolution had been crushed by Mother England, it would be a footnote in history, with the Loyalists being the heroes who helped squash that pesky rebellion. Traitors would be heroes.

We only seem able to define what is right after the war is won. Anime has an interesting way of dealing with this problem, and this is a somewhat personal sentiment, but many endings are left open to interpretation by the viewers - Many times there is no clear winner, or sometimes it appears that everyone has lost somehow. This is very much a mirror of reality...

GOOD PEOPLE CAN DO BAD THINGS.

There are situations that can drive any good person to do something they wouldn't normally do. Anyone can be pushed or persuaded to do something bad, even if it's not in their nature, or against their better judgment. Some of these situations can be brought on by stress, peer pressure, or even necessity. It is a possibility that logic can cause someone to do something bad hoping that they will reach a goal that they perceive to be good.

It is also possible that someone has been raised or taught that something bad is not bad at all, or that if they do a specific thing, that may be bad, it will keep something worse from happening. It is a complicated existence we lead, and sometimes you may need to choose the lesser of two evils. Under the right circumstances it is easy to see how this is possible.

It may still be a moral dilemma, and it may haunt the person afterward, but some decisions in life are painful; and how we handle those decisions is what shows our true character.

SOMETIMES THE BAD GUYS WIN.

Deal with it, life isn't all happy roses and cherry blossoms. It's true; the good guys can't always win. There is a balance to maintain. I guess the good news here is that the bad guys can't always win either. It's a fragile balance that must be maintained; and sometimes it just happens. You have to accept the defeat, move on, and try to do better next time. Hopefully you will have learned something from your defeat, so it won't be a complete loss.

It seems, many times, that the evils of the world are tenacious, cunning, and even appear indestructible... but there is another lesson to be learned here, nothing is indestructible. Be happy about that.

EVIL BASTARDS ARE BEYOND BAD.

There are some guys out there who are not morally righteous. There are some who are selfish. Others are just confused and misdirected. These are not the ones that I'm talking about. I'm talking about fearless, unabashed evil. The ones, who manipulate, destroy, defile, and torture anything and everything others care about. This is generally not a role for women. Remember that there are exceptions, but as a rule, men are the true bearers of destruction. Women give birth to life and men tend to be better at destroying it.

There is no good rule for evil guys, except that there always seems to be someone who's worse. Which doesn't really help; because just when you think you've found the most evil man on the planet, chances are that there's someone right around the corner who makes him look like a boy scout.

If they kill you, that's bad. If they kill your family... that's worse. If they stomp little kittens to death before annihilating the entire solar system... now we're starting to get somewhere.

There are few ways to stop pure evil, and many people would make the assumption that using pure good would be the best solution. That isn't always the case. To make someone good destroy anything, even if it's evil, takes a little bit of doing... it's not in their nature... that's why they're the good guys.

More often than not, it takes a little help from another bad guy; maybe with a guilty conscience or a chip on his shoulder to help this process along. It makes more sense to have evil turn against evil; they are generally selfish anyway...

WAR IS HELL

A relatively common statement, its impact is sometimes lost by the frequency that we hear it. Because most people are not exposed to war on a daily basis, we seem to forget the trauma and suffering that accompany war. War is indeed hell. Sometimes it's not clear what the reasons are for war, or even who the victor is, but there are a great many lessons to be learned here.

THERE IS NO SUCH THING AS A PERFECT STRATEGY.

You can come up with all the plans you want. You can toil over every aspect of an engagement. There is no such thing as a guarantee in war... you try to eliminate risk, diminish casualties, and minimize collateral damage; however, in the fog and chaos that will ensue, you can guarantee nothing.

This is actually more of a life lesson than you think. There is no such thing as a perfect plan. You can't plan everything, mainly because you can't predict everything. There are far too many variables in life. You are better off setting some flexible guides to try to follow, and have a well defined objective. Just like you can't predict the trajectory of a cruise missile to the nanometer, neither can you predict the outcome of any volley, whether in war, life, love or just a heated exchange with a sibling.

If we had the ability to predict every outcome, there would be no use for war. We could just sit back and say who would win and move on. It's the chaos of life that makes everything interesting; we can predict nothing with complete certainty.

You can't even predict the simple things in life. If I made the prediction that my alarm clock will wake me up at *exactly* 6 a.m. because I set it that way... it's certainly a good bet, but it isn't 100%. What if the power goes out, a mouse chews through the cord, I sleep through the alarm, or maybe my girlfriend sets it for a different time without me knowing? There are a lot of variables in life to consider, and that's just waking up.

How can anyone predict the perfect strategy when you have thousands of people with weapons trying to survive and fight for their cause? People are not machines, so reactions in war can be very confusing. People can accidentally attack their own troops, become afraid and withdraw, mistake orders, or even drop their weapon. You can't predict what the outcome will be for something that chaotic.

Now there are certainly statistics and probability. Chances are that 300 soldiers versus 30,000 soldiers will not be a very long conflict, but there have been times in history where the advantages went to the better trained, prepared and just plain lucky; even if they were far fewer in number. This just helps to reinforce the fact that there are exceptions to every rule, and nothing is completely certain in life.

YOU CAN BE AN ARMY OF ONE, OR ONE OF AN ARMY; BOTH ARE IMPORTANT.

Battles in life and war are waged in groups, but these groups contain individuals, and these individuals can sway a conflict one way or another depending on how the chips fall. You can have a single person who can rally troops, boost morale, inspire confidence, and can follow through with resolve and discipline. This one person may be the worst fighter you have, but that person is as important as the one soldier who has killed hundreds by himself.

Just because you aren't the best in a conflict, doesn't mean you have nothing to offer. A group of people in any situation have certain skills and attributes that they have individually developed, and call upon when they need them. People are all different with our varied minds and skills. The one who can pull people together is a skillful person indeed, especially in times of hardship.

The flipside is the army of one; the one who is good at everything, but only works alone. This is an interesting position to be in, because no matter how good you are, you can't defeat the entire universe by yourself. Everyone needs help at some point, in life and war. However the lone soldier is important... they sometimes take the risks that others will not. They are more effective alone anyway. It's a heroic sight to see when the lone warrior accomplishes his mission against great odds.

There's a certain appeal to this type of person. Everyone sometimes feels as if they are alone, and they have to fight off the entire world all by themselves. You can aspire to be like the lone soldier in times of hardship and loneliness. But don't forget to gather your troops when you have them, because it is good to be self-sufficient, but it is also good to be a comrade.

OLD SOLDIERS TELL STORIES FROM EXPERIENCE.

It's always good to listen to those with more experience than you. This is a situation where the lessons won't always save your life, but may help to give you a sense of purpose. Old soldiers don't tell you stories about how to kill, but more tell stories about why they fought. They tell of the good times and bad times, and the responsibility to do your duty, help your friends, and to fight for what you believe in.

War isn't always about the death and destruction, it is more frequently a psychological battle fought in the minds of every soldier serving their duty. There is the anticipation of battle, the urge to be part of something bigger than yourself, and the want to get back home safe... there are a great many issues that you need to deal with internally.

This is the same as with life. Fight for what is important, and for the right reasons. Protect your friends, and support them in times of need. Don't crack under the pressure of life; be strong and resolute. These are all good lessons from the old soldiers, and the good news is... they survived. They faced what may have seemed to be impossible situations and made it home. That is the true inspiration of the old soldier's stories; that you can make it, no matter what you face.

INNOCENT PEOPLE GET HURT.

It's tough to think about death, but it seems less justified when innocents get hurt in a situation they had no control over. Maybe a stray bullet, mistaken identify, bad information or even just an over-zealous soldier in a chaotic situation; people get hurt who aren't involved. This is sometimes unavoidable, and there are attempts made to minimize this phenomenon, but there is a problem with this. War itself is not designed to save those who are innocent; it is designed to win at all costs. Sometimes those costs are in lives that you would rather not lose.

In life, innocent people get hurt all the time. We hurt people without even knowing it. Sometimes we are aware that it is happening, and we try to ignore it, forget about it, or justify it. Other times it occurs without our knowledge, and we can't do a whole lot about that; except to try to think about the consequences of our own actions.

In life we sometimes hurt people in ways you can't see on their skin. You can hurt people's feelings, crush their confidence and self-esteem; you can even turn people over to the enemy's side. These consequences cannot always be predicted, as nothing in life is certain, but there are certain occasions where it's easy to predict that the outcome is going to be bad.

In some situations, it's unavoidable. In other situations, it's unpredictable. But sometimes it is predictable and avoidable, and, in these situations, all precautions should be taken to try to avoid it, as long as it doesn't destroy you. Remember that sometimes you need to obliterate the enemy, and your only option may injure the innocent... it's a tough choice, but if it must occur... God help you and them.

FRIENDLY FIRE IS A FACT OF LIFE.

One of the most difficult issues to deal with is friendly fire. It has a serious psychological effect on morale; to know that you can be turned on by your own side - even if it's accidental. Friendly fire is what happens when you enter a conflict and friendly forces are injured by their own side. It's sometimes difficult to avoid friendly fire injuries in war, and it's even more difficult to avoid it in life sometimes. Now this doesn't mean that you are going to shoot your best friend accidentally, however, there are things that can happen that can cause your best friend some strife.

People can get caught up in situations where their friends can get their feelings hurt if care isn't taken. Sometimes it happens without your knowledge as to why. Let's say you get a new friend, then meet a girl and start dating her... then you find out that it was your new friend's ex-girlfriend. Oops, another friendly fire incident; time for damage control. He's not comfortable with you because you are closely associated with someone who may now be considered the enemy. How do you solve this?

Some situations in war and in life cannot be remedied no matter how hard you try. If you accidentally kill a squad of your own troops, and there is only one survivor... he's probably not going to be too happy with you - no matter what you say. You can make all the excuses you want, you both lose.

You can try to explain that you didn't have enough information, and if you had that information, things may have turned out differently. But there's not a whole hell of a lot you can do about it after the fact to make amends... that's just the way it goes sometimes.

DEAL WITH IT, IT'S OVER - AND LEARN FROM IT.

After a conflict has ended, it is important to move on with your life. The conflict is over. You may have gone through horrors that you never expected, but it's best to find the lessons and learn from them, rather than to dwell on it. General lessons you can apply to everyday life can be learned from anything... just remember that you can't change it after it's done. You can't change your past; learn from it and move on.

Many people who face traumatic events have a difficult time moving on. They are sometimes haunted by the things they have done, choices they have made, or even things that happened to them. It's good to learn the lessons starting with the basics. You are alive, that's good. That means you survived, and that's the most important rule in life... survive. If you don't survive, the life lessons are kind of lost on you.

Now in life, not everything is life threatening... even in war. You may learn about people doing bad things, and do nothing about it. Then later you find out that you should have done something at the time because other people were hurt because you did nothing. Chock it up to a lesson - next time you run into something similar, you will do something. Also, if you survive it, those are the stories you can tell as an old soldier to help people with moral decisions in the future.

If you survive it, it doesn't always make you stronger, but it may make you wiser... and that's better than nothing.

HONOR

In the modern age, many people have become selfish, and in this search for selfish gains, people have lost their sense of honor and valor. These traits are very well documented in the stories portrayed in anime... let's explore them.

DON'T TAKE WHAT ISN'T YOURS.

There are many situations in life where we want things that aren't ours; money, riches, fame, credit, popularity, friends and more. The point is that these things, many times, are not ours for the taking. Honorable people earn what they get; they don't just take it.

WORK HARD.

A good work ethic is an admirable thing. There are so few people who embody the ideals of a good work ethic, and society suffers for it. For every two people who work half as hard as they should, there's one person who has to kill themselves working twice as hard to pick up the slack. This is not an honorable way to live; having someone else pick up your work because you slacked off. Work hard and you will be rewarded.

SHARE WITH THOSE IN NEED.

Charity is a trait that honorable people possess. They help others before themselves. They are not selfish. They give without expecting anything in return. They do not even care to be recognized for their charity. This is real honor. If you give a gift and put your name on it, this may be a subconscious way of trying to get recognition for it... think about it.

CONSIDER THE FEELINGS OF OTHERS, EVEN YOUR ENEMIES.
It is sometimes possible to forget that our enemies have feelings too. Maybe the reason why they are enemies stems from the fact that we don't consider their side of the coin as often as we should. You may gain an enemy for taking a friend away from another, without even knowing it. Pay attention to the reasons why people do things, not just what they do.

SACRIFICE AND COMPROMISE.
There may be problems that are more difficult to resolve than others. In this case there may not be an "everybody wins" scenario. The way to resolve this is to evaluate the situation, define what is important, and then decide what the solution is. This answer may involve giving up something you've worked hard for and obtained honorably, but that action caused hardship and strain... this may have been unforeseeable, but it has now become a problem. Is there a compromise? Can it be shared? Or should you just give it up all together? Maybe you shouldn't have tried for it in the first place. Life is full of these little overlapping dilemmas, and to be able to compromise and sacrifice are some of the only ways that these can be solved.

OVERCOME YOUR FEAR AND DO WHAT IS RIGHT.
There are times in this world when we know what is right but we don't act because of fear. This may be fear of physical or emotional harm. The point is we don't act because we are afraid of what may happen to us. We fear failure, pain, rejection, loss and embarrassment, but to truly do what is right, we need to act honorably and do what is right in the face of any odds. This is the basis for valor; to be a hero, despite the circumstances.

REPAY YOUR DEBTS.

There are times in life when you may become indebted to someone. This is not always monetary; it may be an unselfish act or deed that someone bestowed upon you. You should make every attempt to repay their kindness and generosity. You may feel that you are not able to offer much, but the point is to try. Even if you feel you have nothing, you can offer respect, kindness and gratitude for exchange; and if you offer this with all of your heart, you will find a way to repay your debts eventually.

DEFEND THE HONOR OF OTHERS.

Part of being honorable is defending the idea of honor itself. Part pride and part duty, honor should be defended whenever it's unjustly threatened. People will lie, cheat and belittle others. If you sit there and watch it happen, you are not very honorable. Honor is not always defensible through the use of force, however it does help you to be strong; it's possible that a direct assault will cause more dishonor for the affected party.

Defending honor is a tricky thing, mainly because people have different beliefs, values and ideas. Defeating their enemy in battle may appear to be defending their honor, but maybe it was a battle that they had to win for themselves in order to retain their honor? Perhaps you would have done better to train them in how to win. Helping people defend their honor is the same as defending it yourself.

DON'T DISHONOR YOUR FAMILY.

A family is an important unit in society, and honoring that bond is an important responsibility. A family can be more than just blood bonds; these are also your closest friends that would do anything for you. Do not take those bonds lightly. You have a duty to them to do what is right, and to not bring shame and dishonor to those closest to you.

IT'S ALL IN YOUR MIND...

The brain is one of the most complicated systems on the planet, probably in the universe. It's hard to tell whether or not our own brains are on our side or if they are messing with us like everyone else. Let's get into the mind shall we...

GENIUS CAN COME FROM MORONS.

It's difficult to understand how sometimes the greatest ideas come from the dumbest of people. This isn't always about education either. There are many uneducated people who are geniuses in their own rights. This is a reference to the people who are the dimmest bulb on the tree - if they have any brightness at all. It's possible to over-think a problem; sometimes the solution is staring you in the face, and you're too busy calculating to see it. This is where the morons come in.

They may not be geniuses, but they have moments where their "unique perspective" is the only way to approach a problem. These morons tend to have a carefree attitude, and when everyone's powerful intellect is clouded with the complexities of a situation, these imbeciles are the only ones thinking as clearly as they always do. Many of the best solutions are the simplest ones anyway.

However, this isn't to say that they are spouting genius every time they open their mouths, it just means that you should pay attention to them; you never know when the next pet rock is going to happen. They may only be a pawn in the game of life, but they're sometimes too dumb to come up with anything less than genius.

DREAMS ARE NOT REALITY, BUT THEY'RE NOT NOTHING.

Sometimes you have a dream that seems so real, that you think it must be real. Well it's not. But it's possible that your mind is giving you some subconscious suggestions about how you should handle yourself in the future. Dreams are a good way to sort through feelings, situations, and scenarios that may be difficult or impossible to evaluate when functioning with the conscious mind.

Dreams are the test bed for real thought. We try it out in our sleep, and if it's a good idea, we carry it further with some conscious reflection. The dreams can be a reflection of many different emotions as well. We have dreams of love, fear, hate, futility, embarrassment, violence, serenity, pain and pleasure. Some dreams are there to tie together the feelings that we suppress during the day with our conscious mind.

The conscious mind shuts off when we sleep, so the logic we use to suppress all those emotions is removed and some weird stuff can happen. You can explore what your mind blocks during the day, while you are busy trying to maintain control of your life. It's not often that you have completely random dreams about things you have no experience with; however, it's not always the big things you deal with everyday. It can be a small detail or a moment that haunts your dreams.

Maybe you made eye contact with a person you found attractive. Maybe you slipped and fell in a puddle. Maybe you hit a squirrel with your car. Anything can trigger a dream. Now if all of that happened in one day, you may have a dream about falling in love with a dead squirrel you found in a puddle that a pretty girl stepped in... Who knows? ...but you can lay back and watch the show in your mind. Maybe you'll learn something about yourself that you didn't know.

FLASHBACKS ARE MEMORIES THAT HAPPEN WHETHER OR NOT YOU WANT THEM TO.

It's strange how the mind remembers stuff. It seems that some of the memories we would most like to forget are the ones we remember most vividly. It also seems that the stronger an impact the memory had on our emotions, the better we remember it. The main problem with this comes when some of those emotions get triggered and then the memories associated with them come back as a powerful flashback.

Some flashbacks are good, and some are bad. If you happened to have a very embarrassing situation occur while trying to gain someone's affection, you will probably never forget it; and even worse, you may be reminded with that flashback every time you see that person. Any memory that has a powerful emotional or psychological impact can come back to haunt you. A lot of firsts come back; the first time you saw your girlfriend, the first kiss, the first time you made a complete fool out of yourself, the first time you got into a fight, the first breakup, first time having sex with an alien... the list goes on and on.

The brain sometimes seems to be screwing with us. It seems that if you haven't resolved the psychological effects of a memory, it can be triggered at any time. This may be a way of the brain trying to teach us a lesson. Remember the emotions, and situations in great detail - maybe there's something you need to learn. It almost seems that people function despite the fact that our brains can randomly attack us.

These flashbacks can be of any powerful memory, even if it's an event that didn't actually happen. Maybe it's a dream you had, or something you were told about. Something you heard that didn't seem important, but the situation has caused that memory to resurface. As I stated before, the human brain is a complicated system, and it's not always clear why the brain does this type of thing. Pay attention to your brain though, it's either trying to tell you something, teach you something, or shield you from making another horrible mistake - like the one that caused the flashback in the first place.

FANTASY IS ALWAYS BETTER THAN REAL LIFE.

When our minds take a trip away from reality and we start entering a daydream of fantasy, everything always seems to be perfect. This process is almost always punctuated by the reality that nothing is perfect. There's nothing wrong with fantasy; it's our minds trying to help us visualize what we want. As long as we realize that it isn't reality, it isn't too dangerous to do.

Acting on fantasy is generally interesting in reality, as our fantasies are based on our own perspective and ambitions. You can act on your fantasy, but be prepared. The nice girl, that you thought would be so kind, may have no urge to even look at you. Everyone has their own fantasies, and it's a rare commodity to find the person who's been fantasizing about you, and even rarer to be having the same fantasy as you.

Fantasies do motivate people though. They give you something to look forward to; an attempt to find reasons to act on your feelings. You can try to make your fantasies come true, but you will undoubtedly fall short if you have any imagination at all. Your fantasy may be as simple as kissing that girl at the school dance, or as complicated as taking over the world and being worshipped by all women. This is a great fantasy but not incredibly practical.

The rule of thumb is to dream big, but expect little. This is a way to keep yourself from losing your mind every time your fantasy falls short in reality. But remember that your fantasies are telling you about your deepest urges, listen to them; they are a part of who you are... they are your hopes and dreams.

THE MIND IS INFINITE IN ITS POWER.

Being as complicated as it is, you may think that the brain is capable of anything. Well in short, it is. Anything is possible in your mind. This doesn't mean that it's actually possible in reality, but it's a start. Every great invention was impossible until the brain came up with a way to make it possible. The brain can overcome many of the obstacles that the world places in front of it. The mind is an amazing thing.

Put a few good minds together and you can accomplish almost anything. You may not be able to levitate a bus with the force of your mind, but you can get into a crane and lift one. It is impossible to estimate the limit of the human mind. Some people have the ability to remember all kinds of facts, and others can do any number of complex calculations. The mind is the source for all of our culture, arts, sciences, dreams, emotions, memories, instincts and pain. A body with a broken mind is worthless, but a mind with a broken body can still unravel the most complex mysteries of the universe.

APPEARANCES CAN BE DECEPTIVE.

We use our minds to observe the universe around us, but not all things are as they appear. Your mind tends to see things from a singular perspective... your own. This can make some of the more complicated things in life seem simple. The brain tends to react quickly to new stimuli, and quickly develops an analysis of it. This is sometimes referred to as a first impression... and first impressions aren't just for the first time you meet someone (even though your first impression of the little Chihuahua may be right on); first impressions also occur for any situation that you might find yourself in.

If you walk into your house and see your husband or wife hugging someone of the opposite sex, then your first impression is probably going to need a little more investigation before you jump to any conclusions. This may be a family member you don't know, an old friend, or some other benign situation...

however, it may not. The mind likes to work fast and jump to conclusions; and it can either save your life, or ruin it.

It may be that you have a popular person at school that appears to be good at everything, and they appear to have it all. Athletic ability, money, brains, a good family life... their life must be easy... or is it? Sure the mind would jump to that conclusion because those are all things that you would assume would make your life easy if you had them. You may not see a tormented person who is horrified of failure, and makes themselves sick over every detail of their life. They may appear to have a good family, but it may be overbearing... you just don't know. You assume that everything should be great for this person, because this is how they appear to you.

That's the deception of appearance. Someone can appear happy, and be tormented. They can tell you one thing and be thinking something else. Tell you everything is ok, when their mind is eating them alive from the inside. The minds of some people function in a way that masks their inner feelings to put up the appearance of happiness and stability, even though they are a whirlwind of confusion and doubt.

However, the more you get to know someone, the more you challenge your first impressions... or reinforce them. It's best to not just jump to conclusions and dismiss something as two-dimensional... life is rarely that simple, even though the mind likes to make it seem that way.

GET STARTED... NOW!

CHAPTER 18

There are some people in the world who are interested in anime, but don't know how to get started in watching it. How do you tell what's good and bad? How can you tell what you'll like? Because everyone is different, there is no single rule that applies for everyone... but you can use some of these suggestions as a start.

START WITH THE INTERNET.

You can research movies on the internet; the same is true with anime. Read some reviews and plot descriptions, watch some trailers. Maybe even watch some online. This is a good way to get started without having to dump a whole ton of money.

There are some other internet ideas too, related to the way people judge a movie or series. There is an interesting phenomenon, related to anime, called the Anime Music Video or AMV. Think of it like a movie trailer, where the editor puts together their favorite scenes in a music video format... to any music they choose. The best part of this is that it is usually made by other fans, not corporations or studios, so this shows how other viewers feel about it.

Find some good AMV's with music you like, and find a few different ones based on the same title. See what it looks like. If you like action, then you'll see if it has some. If you like romance, sci-fi, giant robots, pretty girls, or just plain chaos...

you'll see that too. Read up on it. You don't need to spoil it for yourself though... just get an idea and take a chance.

Now think of it from this standpoint, if there are a few hundred different people putting up information about a certain anime; it at least has enough appeal to make a few hundred people post information about an anime, they're not getting paid for. This doesn't mean it's going to appeal to you, but it at least has some merit... it's probably worth a look if it matches your tastes.

LONGER DOESN'T ALWAYS MEAN BETTER... SOMETIMES IT'S A REAL BAD SIGN.

For the true anime fans, this double-entendre has extra meaning. Longer doesn't mean better when selecting your anime. I've seen great stories told in 30 minutes, and I've seen a show that didn't progress at all in like 112 episodes. I'm not going to name any names here, but trust me on this.

It's also a good idea to find out how long it's going to take you to watch this. I understand that most people do not wish to spend a few thousand hours watching something, so this concept might be important to you. There are a lot of different options for that. There are short anime films, short series type, long series, direct to video (called OVA or OAV – Original Video Animation), full feature length movies, and more. This part of the decision is up to you. I would suggest starting with a feature film or a short series to get your feet wet; this gives you a lot of different options for stories over a short period of time.

It's better to follow your feelings on this one. It varies by person. I personally don't know of many stories that can't be told in less than 30 episodes... so I tend to stay away from stuff that goes up to 5 million episodes. I tried it once. It started out strong for about 5 episodes then went into autopilot for the next 60 or so. After talking with a friend about this, he said that I stopped just shy of the episode where stuff starts to happen that relates to the progression of the main story again... Sorry, I wasted enough of my life on that.

YOU CAN'T JUDGE AN ANIME BY ITS COVER, OR TITLE.

Just like you can't judge a book by its cover, the same is true with anime. I have purchased far too much crap that looked good at the time when standing in the store. You should probably research anything that you are going to buy. The marketing of anime is very complicated, so trying to deduce a genre or plot summary through looking at the cover, title, or paragraph on the back of the video can be difficult.

LET THE BATTLE BEGIN, DUBBED OR SUBBED.

Remember that anime is a foreign product (unless you're Japanese.) Just like in foreign movies they have different versions - some with original Japanese soundtracks and dialog, subtitled in different languages, and other versions over-dubbed in other languages. There are different camps involved in the anime world, and everyone has their opinion. The true purists say, "Learn Japanese. Then you don't need subtitles or the butchery of a bad translation with cheesy voice actors." There are others who are sort of pure. They enjoy the original form, but don't quite have the time or capacity to learn Japanese; they usually prefer subtitles. Then there are the people who prefer dubbed; they don't want to read the whole thing, but don't know Japanese, so they focus on the story as a whole, hoping that any weird voice acting or cheesy dialog will pan out in the end.

Then there are people with no preference. Personally, I would love to have the time to learn Japanese so I could have a full selection of all the anime ever made. But I would rather be watching it, than learning Japanese... so that's the dilemma. I will read subtitles if that's the only option, or watch it dubbed if it exists. Sometimes I do both, just to see if there's a difference in the translation - and to see how close the character's voices sound in different languages with different voice actors.

This again is another preference, there are huge debates over which is better. DVD's generally have both the original (with or without subtitles) and dubbed (sometimes in multiple languages.) You have more of an opportunity to choose, now that you are given the options. Some come in full screen and/or wide screen, even others in high definition! It used to be that you would buy a VHS and it would say, "Original Dialog with Subtitles", or "English/other language Dialog." That was it.

This is up to you. If you already know Japanese, then you win... if not, I guess it depends on how well you can read. ☺

BEWARE THE SUPER DEFORMED (A.K.A. WHAT THE CHIBI?)

An interesting artistic expression used in a lot of anime, especially in humorous situations, is the use of a style referred to as super deformed, lovingly referred to as chibi. Chibi means little person or small child. Anime can have some very amazing artwork, but then almost randomly, the character changes form... into a sort of big-headed, midget version of itself with giant eyes. There are actually a great many different types of this.

You can have anything from a full detail, almost life-like portrayal of a character down to a gelatinous blob with dots for eyes. This is most likely done for a couple of reasons. Artistic license, which means they do what they want for whatever effect they were looking for... or more likely cost.

There are a lot of ways to save money in animation. Remove a few lines, details, or colors, from a few thousand frames of animation and you save a whole lot of time and money. This is part of the charm of some anime titles. But you need to be expecting it. If you start watching it and you didn't know that the same character could have 6 different forms in one scene, it may get difficult to follow.

This can be anything from amusing to annoying, depending on how it's done, and how often. Be prepared for it, in case it happens, but don't be concerned, it's not a bad trip or anything.

Some titles do not use this at all, and generally they are the full length, big budget features. This is not always the case though; just a general guideline.

SOME ANIME IS NOT FOR KIDS... AS SOME ISN'T FOR ADULTS, AND SOME IS PERFECT FOR YOUR PERVERTED LITTLE TEENAGER.

There are many different types and genres of anime, like with regular movies and TV shows. Some are for adults because of sex and violence, some are ok for teens with some bad language and some risqué scenes (maybe some nudity) and some are just action scenes for the younger ones. There are some really weird things out there in anime-land and I'm going to cover some of them for you now.

It's hard to tell which titles are 100% appropriate without viewing but here's some stuff to look for, or look out for.

Hentai is pornography in the simple explanation. It can range anywhere from provocative clothing and situations, to aliens with giant tentacles raping and destroying, and performing bondage with animals while pooping on them. There are very few pure hentai films which have anything other than a faint simple plot, but such is the same with regular pornography, I guess.

Ecchi is a sub category of hentai. It's not raw pornography; it's more like movies that would be considered rated R or PG-13, like the old *Porky's* movies or the first *Revenge of the Nerds*. Sexual scenes and nudity can occur but are not the objective. This is generally the arena where we hear the term "fan service." This term refers to anything done solely to keep the fans happy. Lot's of jiggling, partial nudity, showers, baths, beach trips, panty shots, locker rooms and more. Fan service also covers putting in little bits of information that only the true fans would know; like having the director or creator as a character, paying homage to an influence or something like that. Ecchi basically means that it's a little lewd and dirty. This may be acceptable (depending on your parenting style) for kids under 18, if you watch it first and see that it's something they can probably handle. With all the sexually explicit and suggestive behavior in TV and movies today, many of these are charming, innocent, and prude by comparison.

Violence varies in anime. You can have *Tom and Jerry* style violence, where it looks bad but there's not a lot of blood and no one really gets hurt, or you can have graphic butchery and death with blood everywhere. There's a lot of variety in here for that. Some of these are great for everyone, others are definitely not. It's hard to tell sometimes, many of us kids just had parents that thought all cartoons were for kids so they didn't worry about it. I guess I lucked out on that, but I also didn't have the internet to look it up on when I was 8 - trying to spend my allowance on another anime.

Kid's anime is still around, however if you're reading this, then you are probably not going to want most of it. Some of it is pretty trippy stuff, but most of it just isn't that good anymore. Personally, I like the older classic kid's anime that was around when I was growing up. Sure the animation wasn't all that great in some of them, but the stories were a little better I think. Also, I think many of the older kids would like some of that stuff too.

RENT MANY, BUY OFTEN AND TAKE A CHANCE.

There's a lot of anime out there, but you will see a lot of similar storylines if you stick to a single genre; just like if you watched all romantic comedies, or horror movies, you would see a lot of similar stories done a different way. The way to deal with this problem, at least for me, is to take a chance. Rent a lot of different stuff, and see what happens. If you take this approach, you may find a direction to go in. Then after you rent the first DVD of a series, you may go buy the boxed set... or just give up on it altogether. Renting is a good way to try before you buy... but if you like it, I would suggest buying it. Remember, if it isn't profitable to release a whole bunch of different titles because no one's buying them... then they won't release them.

FRIENDS DON'T LET FRIENDS LIVE WITHOUT ANIME.

After you get into it, pass it on. You'll find that sharing this is an interesting ice breaker. You may run into people who have never seen an anime before, and you can run into people like me who have seen more than they care to try to fathom. Find some good anime and start them out as you got started... if you know them fairly well, then you can judge what they might like.

Maybe even give them a copy of this book to help them get started!

Then you'll end up as an otaku, dressing up for cosplay in no time! Baka! Baka! Baka! Baka! Baka! (I told myself I wouldn't do that!)

SOME CLOSING THOUGHTS

It would be impossible for me to mention and explain all of the lessons to be learned from anime, as it would be equally uninteresting. Everyone has a different perspective; how I see and interpret the lessons is probably different from the next person... mainly because we are all different...

Even if you are one of the triumvirates...

There are great epic stories to be told... there are more shallow ones as well. All of them have a place for someone... somewhere. I cannot calculate or estimate the amount of anime I have absorbed up to this point of my life, as I'm sure many of you out there cannot, but I also can't say that I'm any more an expert on anime than anyone else.

I've watched it... lots of it, and I have a learned a few lessons from it that I wanted to share - that's why I wrote this book in the first place.

I would suggest watching as much as you can stomach - you'll find ones you love, ones you hate, others you want to emulate; they make us laugh, cry, jeer, scream, smile, wince, and cheer. Just remember it's only anime... and that in itself makes it glorious.

All people who watch anime have their favorites and they love to tell everyone what they are, so here are some of mine, just for the record...

Akira, Jin Roh, Ninja Scroll, The Hakkenden, The Wings of Honneamise, Vampire Hunter D, Battle Angel, Patlabor 1, Golgo 13: The Professional, Steamboy, Fist of the North Star, Wicked City, Ghost in the Shell, Ai Yori Aoshi, and the greatest story ever told - Robotech.

Later - Sid

Printed in the United States
208542BV00004B/2/P